THE
JAPANESE
CHRONICLES

Also in English by Nicolas Bouvier

The Way of the World

The Scorpion Fish

THE
JAPANESE
CHRONICLES

BY

NICOLAS BOUVIER

TRANSLATED BY ANNE DICKERSON

Polygon
EDINBURGH

English translation copyright © 1992 by Mercury House, Incorporated
All rights reserved.

Originally published in France under the title Chronique Japonaise © 1989
Editions Payot
Grateful acknowledgement is made to Lucien Stryk for his translation of
Bashō in *On Love and Barley: Haiku of Bashō* (University of Hawaii Press, 1985)

This edition published in 1995 by
Polygon
22 George Square
Edinburgh
Great Britain

Text design: Ann Flanagan Typography
Printed and bound in Great Britain by
Page Bros Ltd, Norwich, Norfolk

A CIP record for this title is available.

ISBN 0 7486 6192 1

The Publisher acknowledges subsidy from the

THE SCOTTISH ARTS COUNCIL

towards the publication of this volume.

. . . When even what passes before our eyes
gives way to the most misleading rumors—
so much more so for a country that lies beyond
eight layers of white clouds.

UEDA AKINARI
(1732–1809)

Dozing on horseback,
Smoke from tea-fires
drifts to the moon

BASHŌ
(seventeenth century)

CONTENTS

ILLUSTRATIONS

All photos by the author

THE GRAY NOTEBOOK

———————●———————

Kyoto, February 24, 1964
Looking for lodging

L ATE AFTERNOON, a stately old home, somber and beautiful, somewhere southeast of the city beyond Uji. An old couple, penniless landlords, who rent a wing of their immense home. He is a distinguished skeleton, with a worn tweed jacket over a gray flannel shirt that looks like a convict's work shirt. And she too is withered, her eyes sunken and feverish, a face like paper-thin silk framed by the collar of a severe and sumptuous kimono. We are sitting cross-legged, in the center of a freezing room around a brazier where a little bitter tea steeps over three embers. Beyond the sliding doors are a small pond and a numbed garden where not a single leaf is trailing. Impossible to tell if it is raining or snowing, but you know that spring will not come tomorrow. The rock, the moss, the wood, the patina of straw mats shined by slippers and reflecting the winter sky—"I love to hear the sounds of a child in the house," says the old man, breaking a long silence to which he quickly returns, while the two women (there is also an attendant or a very proud, very stubborn daughter-in-law) bow slowly. An impression of visiting the home of the dead, the home of the drowned who have just come up from the bottom of the sea. Since we have been here, the real estate agent who brought us has been agitated, snorting, falling all over us although he has known us scarcely an hour, praising this impractical and ghostly house, acting sociable when it means no more than breathing loudly through his gold-filled teeth. No one is listening and no one is worrying about it. How these somber, likable, perfectly composed people must feel to have to negotiate with this kind of swine!

... The cold, heavy cold, its importance in life here can be heard in the jingling of the Japanese music—and the trees! their branches, twisted and angular, as if suffering cramps, as if the cold is mixed into them. And all the poses of the body, as in the theater or in engravings: tight gestures pulled toward oneself, whose only purpose is to prevent the warmth of the body from escaping . . .

The taxi that was supposed to wait for us has disappeared. Walking back up the street I found the driver dozing in a small grocery between jars of sour cabbage and pickled turnips that were steaming in the falling night.

Return to Kyoto by a road that I had followed on foot eight years ago. In six or seven weeks of walking I had come down from Tokyo to this point by following the ancient imperial road; today it goes through country fields. Nights spent beneath the roofs of little temples in the countryside, hamlets and lonely rice fields of the Ki peninsula: I arrived at the outskirts of the old capital an amazed vagabond, which is how you should approach a city of six hundred temples and thirteen centuries of history. I remember it as if it were yesterday: warm June rain, tall, pale-green foliage swaying against a luminous gray sky. Today these same trees are dusted by snow. In the interval between these two journeys, I feel I have somehow been absent from my life. I am curious to see which is more changed—this country or me.

PART ONE

———————•———————

THE
MAGIC
LANTERN

YEAR ZERO

———————●———————

ANYONE TODAY could find the Japanese islands on a map with his eyes closed. But not so many know how the archipelago came to be there, or just where the Japanese came from.

They dropped from the sky.

That, at least, is what we are told in the *Kojiki* (Collection of Ancient Things) and the *Nihongi* (Japanese Chronicles), the most important of the Shinto sacred books, which contain ancient national myths gathered by imperial order at the beginning of the eighth century A.D.

The way in which a people explain their existence may be as informative as the way they live it. Here then, sketching this bizarre cosmogony in broad strokes, rough and raw, is how the Japanese fell to earth, which is the first story they are told.

According to this Genesis, in the beginning was not the "Word," but a layer of ooze floating serenely in the darkness. The subtle and the solid separate to form a High and a Low. Wandering about in this High is a succession of divine spirits (*kami*), orphans without descendants. They don't really do anything because there is no support yet for their actions.

In the Low, all is fluid. There is not even a place to set foot until one day when two *kami* of this first era decide to stir the ocean of silt with the tip of a spear. These *kami* are brother and sister, the creators of Japan, and every Japanese schoolchild knows their names: *Izanagi* (he who courts) and *Izanami* (she who courts). The churned-up sea thickens and a lump drops from their spear and forms the first islet of the Inland Sea. The brother and sister alight on it, look at each other, she entices him, and oh!...they *court*. They join "their majestic parts in a majestic union" and produce three stunted children, because it wasn't seemly for a woman to make such advances. (In all things, the Japanese male is a little slower.) They try again the proper way, in the presence of a wagtail that taps out a beat with its tail, and this time the sister-wife gives birth to the eight islands of Japan. (So there are eight divinities incarnate, fruits of a coupling begun without suffering, remorse, or shame, and the woman has been relegated to the background, with that pretense of submission that has allowed her to pull the strings so conveniently. The bird/metronome rates better than our serpent, I think.)

After producing numerous divine offspring, the goddess gives birth to the Kami of Fire, who burns her so badly that she dies. Her husband-brother, in tears, goes to the realm of shadows to search for her. As in the myth of Orpheus, she promises to follow him back on one condition: he must not look back. But he is anxious and looks at her: he sees a rotten cadaver whose every organ shelters an evil spirit. Furious to have been discovered in this state, Izanami sets all the harpies of the underworld upon her brother-husband. He escapes, driving them away by throwing peaches at them (that's why peaches are considered lucky) and then finally, panting, breathless, he plugs up the opening of hell with a rock.

From the other side of this barrier, the horrible voice of his sister warns him: "So, my fine elder brother, since that's how it is, I will strangle a thousand among your offspring every day."

"Since that's how it is, my sister, I will give birth to five hundred thousand every day." (Take the metro in Tokyo on a Sunday in May and you will see that he has kept his word.) Then, to show her that he means what he says, he spits and begets the Kami of Spit.

Not losing a minute, he goes to purify himself, rinsing off the pollutions of hell in a stream. Every piece of clothing he sheds becomes a *kami* and his scrubbing creates others: *Susano wo* (the Impetuous Male) comes out of his nose; from his right eye comes the Goddess of the Moon; and from the left (in China and Japan, left prevails over right), *Amaterasu O-mi Kami,* Goddess of Light, ancestor of the imperial family and the most venerated figure in the immense Shinto pantheon.

Then, for the first time, the sun rises on a Japan where the great laws of life (you are born, you die, you grow anyhow) have already been given their justification.

The celestial *kami* put *Susano wo,* the Impetuous Male, in charge of governing the Earth; to everyone's dismay, he is soon behaving like a troublemaker, an outlaw, and a hooligan. He destroys the rice growers' dams, puts the horses out to graze in the rice paddies, lays waste to the fields, and releases a flood that kills everyone who doesn't have a solid grasp on eternity. Unhappy at being exiled to the Low, he smears his sister's palace with his excrement, defiles it with the corpse of a colt, creates trouble, and makes himself hateful in a hundred ways. The goal of this excess (the details would fill pages) is probably to force the unwilling Heaven to pay attention to his terrestrial kingdom. So this conflict is necessary, and the god's excesses as well. The numerous temples that still honor him today clearly prove that no one holds a grudge against him. More than a spirit who is truly evil, he is the expression of the Earth's elemental energies, the noisy advocate of an untamed nature in which "even the rocks, trees, and grasses are overtaken by the violence," the expression of an infant world that needs all the celestial forces in order to find its equilibrium and form. But he goes too far, and Amaterasu, offended by these provocations, hides in a cave, plunging Creation into night and the celestial *kami* into confusion.

The *kami* assemble before the cave. They hold interminable discussions on how to lure the goddess from her cave. The story of this assembly is unintentionally funny because one can see, in a primitive form, the horror the Japanese have of the unexpected and the decisions it requires. These *kami* are the rough masters of a still-young universe. They may always be ready to enthusiastically embody a constellation, or a mountain, or thunder, but speculation and strategy are not their strong points. They ask the Kami of Thought to formulate a plan: despite the talent attributed to him,

he proposes one that seems dreadfully vague. They must restore harmony to the world, be sensitive to delicate feelings, and vanquish doubt. In Japan—even celestial Japan—a plan like this is not easy to put into action. Finally, on the expert's advice, the celestial *kami* construct a mirror, send it up to the heavens on the back of a stag, and decorate the trees with peace offerings. They make all the birds sing at once so that the offended goddess will think another sun has risen and to pique her jealousy. But all their schemes fail, and the cave stays obstinately closed.

In a final act, the Goddess of Laughter performs a sacred dance before the group of *kami;* quickly carried away by the rhythm, she picks up her skirts like a bacchanal, exhibiting a good bit of herself. There is a gigantic burst of laughter from the spectators, which brings the intrigued Amaterasu out of her retreat. Her brother, who has made his amends, is sent back to Earth, and Creation continues in the returned light.

Germination everywhere. In the world of the *kami,* everything is born from something, nothing is ignoble. Everything has a divinity—breath, blood, saliva, excrement—and can create other beings, who gradually take up residence in the material world and purge it of its tempers. There are myriads, celestial and terrestrial. Grand and modest. Powerful and subordinate, bearers *in partibus* of a volcano or a shrub. Some acquire a solid base in mythology, and others, after having rendered some slight service, go up in smoke. All that is needed is enough of them to animate all useful or edible things (Kami of the Comb, the Gourd, the Clam, the Rice); to sanctify every natural force; to impregnate every inch, every stump, every stream on Japanese soil; to provide a divine patron to every profession (Kami of the Distillers and even of the Spies!) and to every future clan of humans; and to neutralize the evil forces that climb from a still-turbulent matter and "swarm like flies on the May moon."

To ensure order, the goddess Amaterasu sends her grandson Ninigi, armed with a saber, a jewel, and a magic mirror, to take earthly affairs in hand. Descending to the island of Kyūshū, the

young prince meets a mountain spirit who offers him his help and
the hand of his eldest daughter: she is a repulsive winter spirit, but
she can grant immortality. He refuses her and chooses the beautiful, younger daughter instead, and so he wins the right to die. (In
this way Heaven joins Earth, and this is why the sovereigns of
Japan, despite their illustrious ancestry, die like all their subjects.)

Two generations later, Jimmu Tenno, the first human emperor,
conquers Yamato and founds the Japanese state. To be very precise
(that is, to be very mythological), on February 11, 660 B.C.

For a long time, the Japanese, honestly convinced of the excel-
lence and uniqueness of their divine nature, will not be able to consider people who come from outside anything other than "foreign
devils." For a long time, the natural reaction of a foreigner will be
to ridicule this potpourri of national legends as incongruous, infan-
tile, absurd, or indecent. In the eighteenth century, the German
traveler Kaempfer, informed as well as he could be of the national
origins, concluded "that in brief the entire system of Shinto gods
is such a ridiculous weaving of monstrous and unacceptable fables
that even those whose business it is to study them are ashamed to
reveal the ineptitudes to the members of their own sect and still
more so to the Buddhists or members of some other religion." And
I guess you will easily believe him.

A question of customs and climate. After all, a Man-God born
to a Virgin in a stable, kept warm by an ass and a cow, and nailed
to two beams between two thieves by the will of a merciful
Father . . . Put yourself in the place of the first Japanese who heard
this story so familiar to us!

Kaempfer adds that he cannot find in this mythology "anything
that could satisfy the questions of the curious about the essence
and nature of the gods. . . . " Not much logic and no tragedy, it is
true. But he forgets:

—No sin: pollutions, and purifications to get rid of them.

—No mortification: "cleansing," for one is to reflect like a clear
mirror on the happy organization of things.

—No ethics or morals, since the "divine" origin of the Japanese dictates their course to them; instead, ceremonies, rituals, and instructions.

—No doctrine or "reasonable proof," but litanies where one enumerates in the same breath the gods and the gifts that they assure you:

> *August Kami of the Crossroads*
> *Kami of the Metalliferous Mountain*
> *of Clay*
> *of the Right Hand*
> *of Thermal Springs*
> *of the Rice Grain*

Litanies chanted every day in the sanctuaries, which sound like a moderately rich man (Japan is a frugal country) counting and recounting his few coins in awe and gratitude.

—No *De Profundis,* because when a beneficent spirit listens to you from within a tree trunk or a rock, your first thought is to thank it for being there, then to ask for a little something in passing.

—No chastisement, no Passion, no anguish, no Hell, nor any of the other bearers of evil, except for a handful of dull vagabond Spirits that you appease with a prayer and a few rice balls.

Truly a strange religion!

In that case, what's left "to satisfy the questions of the curious"? There remains the lively story of this agreement slowly negotiated between a benevolent Heaven and her earthly descendants, and the uninterrupted imperial descent that testifies to it. Beyond that there is a deep, undefined gratitude that is not expressed in dogmas but is danced almost daily in the Shinto sanctuaries to the sound of drum, flute, *koto* (a harp lain flat), and a small mouth organ. It is a strange, slow music that seems to be drawn up from the earth, from the black of the roots, of the trunks; beside it any Western requiem (polyphonically much superior) takes on a manufactured, worldly air. Perhaps not as varied or harmonious to our ears, which are accustomed to richer sauces, but with such immediate power that you have to check that the trees under which you are sitting are not running off on the road to Amaterasu's Great Temple in Ise.

From these origins of long ago until the defeat of 1945, the imperial person will know many vicissitudes, but official doctrine will never cease to maintain that "His Gracious Imperial Majesty descends from the goddess Amaterasu, whose virtues, etc." and that the Japanese people were born of divine essence. In the interval, all the outside influences that will reach Japan will find a sky, a soil, and a mentality impregnated with omnipresent *kami,* both rough and easygoing, with whom everything must be shared.

THE ISLAND OF
THE WA

———————●———————

F EBRUARY 11, Kigen-Setsu, the Festival of Origins, celebrates
the foundation of the state in the year 660 B.C. by an emperor
of divine descent. This is a religious truth and that, in itself, is
enough. So why this date with its pedantic precision and nothing
to support it? We must remember that in this part of the world
and at this time, the Chinese are the only ones who keep their
books up-to-date.

It is through the chronicles of the Han and then the Wei dynasties
that Amaterasu's heirs pass from mythology to history. Reports are
rather rare, because China, sheltered by its recently completed
Great Wall, is more directed toward its own immense interior spaces.

Besides, the sea that separates China from Japan is one of the
worst in Asia, and the Chinese are not very good navigators . . . but
such merchants, and so curious! In the second century B.C., risk-
ing everything, they set sail and land in Kyūshū to see if there isn't
some way to sell, buy, or exchange a little something. They call
the country the "Island of the Wo" or "Wa" (which can be read:
dwarves) and note that it is divided into a number of small kingdoms often controlled by "priestess queens" who exert their authority by magic and divination; some of them acknowledge themselves
as vassals of the Han.

Not a hint of those "majestic events" that, according to Japanese
mythohistory, would have stunned the country many centuries
before. Nor of a unified power, much less an absolute sovereign.
Had the Chinese gotten wind of a "Country of the Gods" and of a

"Divine Emperor," they would surely have delighted in this comic pretension, since for them there is only one Celestial Empire: China. And only one Son of Heaven: the emperor Han, who rules the Five Seas and the Four Directions by Heaven's command. No one knows what profit the Chinese bring back from their voyage, but soon the Wa, who are good sailors, return the favor by indulging in raids and trade on the coast of Korea. In A.D. 57, they send a real delegation to China, the first definite scouting party for a long series of exchanges that permit the Chinese to make the following observations:

The emissaries from Wa have arrows with points made of bone; they wear full tunics made of mulberry bark, stiff, heavy, and good-looking. Their manner is fierce and proud, except when they get drunk on rice alcohol, something to which they seem inclined.

And, later:

The Wa have a virgin empress who is a sorcerer. She lives barricaded amongst her servants so that no man can approach her. When the empress dies, a hundred men follow her to her grave. They consult the oracles by holding the shoulder blade of a stag over a fire (a practice that has spread throughout all of central Asia) *and their soothsayers are hairy and dirty. Wa sailors tattoo their bodies to frighten away sea monsters when they dive for seashells.*

Unfortunately, we must report that among the Wa, the dead have only a single thickness to their coffins, and the funerary rituals are quite hasty. (Obviously, the care and attention with which the Chinese bury their dead would be inconceivable to the Shintoists because of the resulting pollution.)

Later still, in the 5th century:

They know the art of sericulture and ricegrowing, but they have almost no water buffalo . . . (Their longevity . . . Their drunkenness . . . And the wonderful way they dress, as if their sure sense of style bothers the Chinese in a people they consider fairly uncivilized subjects. This is the first mention of the artistic sense of the Japanese, who will become the most aesthetic people in the world.)

In A.D. 478, a letter in beautifully written Chinese is sent to the Chinese court by the "king of Yamato, protector of Korea." It is the first text of Japanese origin preserved by history.

By that time, the Wa people had made some progress. The foundation of the state by the emperor Jimmu probably corresponds to the conquest of the Yamato by one of the most powerful clans of Kyūshū, at the very beginning of our era. Western and Japanese historians (except the Shinto) roughly agree on that. Unification is pursued. The raids on the three kingdoms of Korea have placed a kind of protectorate on one of these states, and this allows the Japanese to extract a great deal of knowledge from their unfortunate protégés. Between the fourth and the sixth centuries, there is a close relationship, and Korean convoys make the trip to Japan laden with artisans—sericulturalists, distillers, blacksmiths, weavers, leather tanners, and ceramicists—scholars, and books, all with the character of "technical assistance." Among other valuable gifts: Chinese writing, the first analects of Confucius, and Buddhism, which we will rediscover much later. The arrival of a dressmaker is given as a momentous event.

The Japanese didn't waste a bit of this treasure. They didn't waste any time either. Once jogged into motion, Japan gave the first proof of its amazing power of assimilation and quickly put it to work. The imperial chancellery crammed, learning the ideograms and looking for ways to use the Chinese conceptions of society and power to consolidate their own authority.

In A.D. 607, when the excellent emperor Shōtoku-Taishi (you can see his picture today, his hair in swirls around his face, on every thousand-yen bill) sends a solemn ambassador to the court of China, he has several reasons to be proud of himself: he is a scholar, a fervent Buddhist, a virtuous and popular administrator, and the uncontested lord of a country that has already demonstrated its architectural genius in building the admirable temple of Hōryū-ji near Nara. The letter that he has the ambassador deliver to the emperor Yang-ti is addressed: "From the Emperor of the Rising Sun to the Emperor of the Setting Sun." Its recipient is favorably disposed, but, all the same, this is an eye-opener: it is the first time a neighboring state is treating China as an equal. It takes all the Japanese ambassador's skill to arrange things: good Chinese scholar that he was, he knows very well that his country had borrowed this entitlement from China, without asking for the "patent." After some beating around the bush, the emperor Yang-ti sends the ambassador home laden with presents and carrying a kind letter that puts things back in their proper place. The ambassador thinks it advisable to lose this message at sea—unlikely as that seems— and his master, who easily guesses why, does not hold it against him. And besides, it is inconceivable to quarrel with a China that was entering the T'ang epic, the most brilliant and best-organized empire the world had ever known.

Several years later, the Japanese send another delegation, eight scholars chosen with extreme care for their character, their hunger for knowledge... and above all their virtue, because the sea is dangerous and the Japanese have this beautiful idea that a ship filled with "honorable men" has a better chance of arriving safe and sound. You can imagine the contacts Europe would have established with the ancient and the new world if the navigators of the sixteenth century had been chosen in this manner. It is true that they were not sent to study but to plunder.

The first imperial genealogies were established in the fifth century. It's easy to understand now why their chroniclers recoiled into the night at the beginning of their dynasty. They filled the void by giving the successors of the emperor Jimmu the longevity of the Hebrew patriarchs and adding the occasional intercalary sovereign whose reign is a blank. Maybe it was the natural need to ease the passage from an "august eternity" to our lives, which are surrendered so easily to a case of smallpox, or to the next tile torn by a—

divine—wind from the roof of a temple. But it was probably so it wouldn't blush before its elder, China, that this culture, younger than our own, has granted itself a few more centuries.

A nation that counts its generations back to primordial chaos cannot admit to having been outdone.

"MY LAW WILL SPREAD TOWARD THE EAST..."

(The Word of Buddha)

———————●———————

IN 557 B.C., Siddhartha Gautama (later known as Sakyamuni Buddha), son of the king, was born in a small court in Nepal and immediately shocked the midwives who delivered him by giving them the most pertinent advice.

After years of meditation, he suddenly realized that this world is no more than an illusion to which we are enchained by our appetites, and he taught the Eight Ways to break away from them, to escape from the cycle of reincarnation, and to rest in the peace of nirvana (the place where nothing breathes again). Having preached respect for all life, left his sermons (sutra), and gathered his disciples, he died, and all of creation was filled with sorrow—plants, insects, people, and animals assembled to stand vigil over the body. All except the cat, who preferred to "go about his business" that day, and so in all of Buddhist Asia, to this day, the cat enjoys a reputation as a scoundrel.

A thousand years later, or nearly, in A.D. 552, the emperor of Japan, Kimei, in his palace in Azuka (south of Nara) unpacks the presents that the king of Korea has just sent him. Among the silks, he finds many rolls of Buddhist scriptures, then unwraps a gilded bronze statue of the Buddha. He examines it, "bounding with joy," according to the *Nihongi*, "and asserts that nothing like the grave dignity of this Buddha has ever been seen before."

By this single remark, which so candidly illuminates the essence, the emperor Kimei proves that Japan of the sixth century is definitely deserving of the gift that it is given.

Between these two events, Buddhism has flourished. Driven out of India after several centuries, it reaches central Asia via Tibet or Afghanistan, having been enriched on the way by Hellenistic, Zoroastrian, Tantric, Chinese, even—who knows—Nestorian Christian influences.

In A.D. 64, the Chinese emperor Han is converted.

In the fourth century, it is Korea's turn. Then, at the end of its voyage, the Good Law reaches the farthest country, Japan.

Enriched by all the alluvium collected along its route, Buddhism had become a many-faceted doctrine, inconceivably complex and rich, ranging from the crudest piety to the most dizzying metaphysical speculations. All aspects of Asian spirituality are contained in it, in one form or another.

Along with those gifts to the Japanese emperor, the Korean king has attached a letter that says, in substance: "Of all the known doctrines, this is certainly the best. The merits it will introduce are unlimited, and it will leave no desire unsatisfied." But he adds that it is also the most difficult to grasp, that even Confucius and the duke of Tchou (a Chinese Solomon) probably hadn't understood it a bit, but that all the nations of Asia are joining up nevertheless.

The emperor Kimei is joyous but mystified. To surpass the famous duke of Tchou in wisdom... that is worth considering. And a doctrine so very difficult must be remarkable... but is it really necessary to honor this new god? For his part, he abstains from deciding. And his advisors are divided: the great Shinto priests, who are holding on to their monopoly, threaten him with the vengeance of the *kami;* but their enemies, the Soga clan, who can already see a way to weaken their Shinto rivals with this piece of bronze, advise him to do what China has done, to "go with the times." Rival ambitions.

Finally, the emperor Kimei compromises, bestows the statue on the Soga, and demands that they create a special cult for it. They build a small temple, send for a Korean monk... and then a plague breaks out. The Shinto clan is triumphant—to stop the epidemic, they throw the statue into a smelly canal where, it seems, it refuses to sink.

Twenty years later: the second coming of the saintly images, the texts, and the bonzes (the monks). The Soga, who had not had any qualms about using Buddhism to achieve power, rebuild the temple, and scarcely have time to settle three young nuns there in the idol's service when a second epidemic breaks out. The temple is razed, down to its foundations, the statues take a second bath, and the nuns are stripped and publicly flagellated.

Then the Soga defeat their enemies. The emperor, who was hindering them, "is slaughtered like a cow." They take power, erect a temple to celebrate the success of their crimes, and Buddhism—ironically —receives its license from this group of rogues. But that is just one incident.

The Good Law is established. The grafted stem has taken hold, and Prince Shōtoku, who according to legend was born (A.D. 573) in the straw of a stable—like Christ—tends it carefully. He copies the sutras in gold ink on black paper sprinkled with silver, and he has entire books and statues shipped from Korea. A century later, Nara is under construction. Only monks and workmen are in sight. Immense beams made of cryptomeria wood are poised in the sky, and the recitation of the Law punctuates the work of the roof builders. For the plan, they followed a model of Chinese dimensions, and the huge buildings are a little too big for their site. In the new capital, the acres of glazed tiles sparkle in the sun. The roofs of the temples are larger than a rice field and the astonished peasants measure them in days of work. The beams are gigantic, and the imperial residence looks like a pavilion next to it.

Six sects have already sprung from the interpretation of the scriptures, and on ceremonial days, their priests wear tunics of raspberry, saffron, pistachio, or violet, which create a lovely effect on the gray-brown-green of the Japanese landscape.

Because it is "cultured," Buddhism now calls the tune for everything that comes from Korea and China. The bonzes have their hands in everything: imperial chancellery, astrology, medicine, divination, poetry, and political machinations. They are exempt from taxes, and much dreaded, since the mantras (magic words) are known to kill or cure.

From the Parthian empire, which has already vanished, the

imperial treasury receives brocades decorated with startled ibex; it had taken them a century to make the trip. And in the street, one out of ten passersby is an "expert" from Korea or China; the court pays them to stay for three years.

This Buddhism is a bracing mixture of frenzied labor, cunning, and true devotion. (How I would have loved to see it before the electrical wires and the revolving neon signs of Nara-Dream-Land!)

From contact with this incredible thirst for knowledge and this dynamic culture with a past of its own, Buddhism changes. It is rounded out; some of the abstraction and the Indian pessimism evaporate.

"All life is suffering," said Sakyamuni. But for the Japanese of the seventh century, life is more of an enormous school where one learns something every day—twenty Chinese ideograms, the name of a new star, the recipe for a fumigant, or a medicinal method. Into this ground—however "illusory"—of Nara, the doctrine of renunciation plunges its strong and hungry roots. What is left of the temples of this epic suggests not so much detachment as triumphal affirmation. And Buddhism implants itself in death too, which Shintoism had left to lie fallow. (Not the death of the ancestors, no, but the death of people close to you, death that's feared and mourned.) The bonzes have a consolatory ritual to put you in your grave, and on prescribed dates, they read the sutras on the tomb to pacify the departed souls. Of course, these services cost money.

The cemeteries are the fish ponds for the temples.

From the immense range of Buddhist preaching, the Japanese choose the least somber lessons, those that best satisfy their strong desire to reconcile all things. The priests of the Kegon sect profess that true reality is a final harmony from which nothing escapes. The name of the doctrine? The Doctrine of Total Mutually and Interdependently Relative World Harmony. With a program like that, no one will be left out!

The *kami*, in particular. Except for personal quarrels, these two religious forms seem to live well together. Besides, they serve different ends, so they can easily be juxtaposed. And the Japanese are

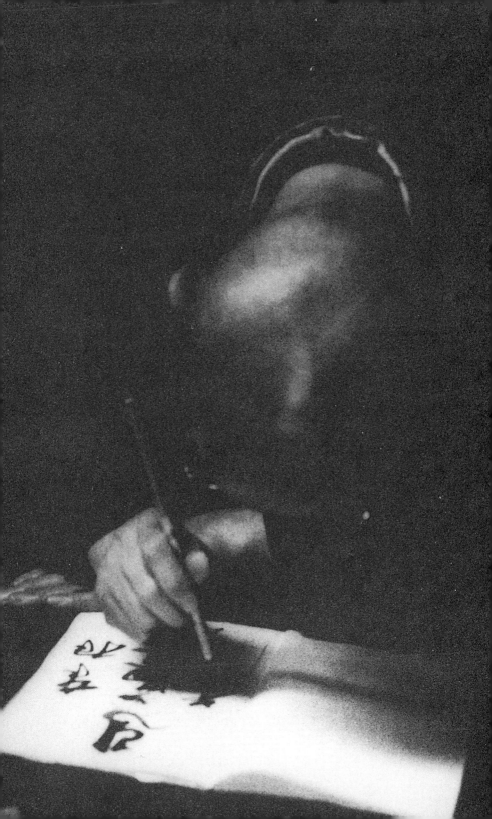

very careful not to let their national gods lose face. So when the emperor levies a tax to pay for the metal and the casting of the Great Buddha of Nara, he sends a very learned bonze to the sanctuary of Ise to explain it to Amaterasu, Goddess of the Sun, so she won't take offense. She tells the messenger in a dream that far from being offended, she is flattered, since she herself is a temporary incarnation of the eternal Buddha. This should not be seen as a cheap fraud on the part of the monk, but rather as evidence of his deep conviction that two such excellent beings have to get along. It is the genius—so Japanese—of compromise. Before very long these two totally different religions of the Japanese will become one, the *ryobu-shinto,* which will have its hour of glory.

During the fifteen centuries that they have coexisted, the Shinto deities and the Buddha have never been in open conflict, and in the gardens of the Buddhist temple, you will always find—in the bush, behind the well, next to the gardening shed—a small Shinto sanctuary decorated with fresh flowers, a sign that the Ancient Proprietor has never really left his place.

THE DREAM OF
AN AUTUMN NIGHT

———————●———————

Heian-kyō (Kyoto), A.D. 1000

IN THE COURTYARD of the quarter where the young empress's
maids of honor live, there is an intruder, a frantic man. He is
rather poorly dressed. He knocks his head on the ground and cries
that an imperial storehouse has burnt down and the fire has spread
to his house, and now he has nothing left and nowhere to sleep.
He isn't speaking to anyone in particular. Obviously he has lost his
mind to make such disjointed speeches to these women of quality.
But these young women lead such an isolated life that the spectacle
of this coarse fellow, especially in the state he's in, is comic and
"interesting." A stroke of luck. Quickly they pull out writing cases
and brushes... then they offer him the clever and sarcastic couplets they have just composed about his misadventure, laughing
all the while. He accepts them with a stupid look: plainly, he
doesn't know how to read.

Not one of these young maidens dreams that, in this situation, a
small coin might please him. (In a corner of the picture, to the left
of the court, there is a roof of blue enamel tiles. This good-luck blue
traveled from ancient Iran to China, Korea, Japan; it lightens the
spectacle of the city marvelously, but the Japanese—who find it too
cheerful for their rainy skies—will soon change it to a silver gray.)

Not one of those small coins pierced with a square hole so that
they can be strung on a string... The man has disappeared, and
one of the young maids of honor records the incident under the
heading "Amusing Things" in her journal, which has survived. Her
name is Sei Shonagon; she has the sharpest tongue of the court; to
kill time, she writes about the trifles that make up her life as a
court attendant. Chinese-style, she entertains herself by recording

"Exciting Things," "Pleasant Things," or "Extremely Annoying Things." Thus:

It is pleasant during the cold winter nights to lie with one's lover under a mountain of quilts. The simple sound of a bell seems so strange then: as if it came from the bottom of a well . . .

By contrast:

When a gentleman leaving you at dawn says that he has left his fan somewhere and starts to bustle around the dark room, bumping into everything and mumbling: "How strange!"—that is very annoying.

And she is not the only one to make a note of what she feels: other ladies of the court keep witty, bitter, or malicious records of the closed world in which they live and create—unwittingly—the first masterpieces of Japanese literature. It is thanks to them that one knows a little about how the leisure class of Heian-kyō spent their lives.

Heian-kyō means "peace and tranquillity."

The city already has three hundred thousand inhabitants. It was founded nearly two centuries before, laid out on a rectangular grid like the Chinese capitals, on a site that the seers had carefully chosen.

Three centuries earlier they had borrowed the lunar calendar from China, adding an intercalary month when they needed it. In the literature of this period there is no talk of the sun, that braggart, that buffoon. The moon is sovereign; she can win hearts, and when she is full, she can make your wish come true. Watching her rise above a well-chosen landscape (*tsuki-mi*) is—still today—one of the favorite pastimes in September.

. . . Among the festivals of flowers, the plum tree follows the festival of the rose, the iris, the azalea; then comes the Festival of Tanabata, which celebrates the conjunction of the Shepherd's Star and the Spinner's Star. October is the time of the maple tree; its reddening leaves begin to distract the bonzes chanting in their

temples. The whole year revolves around flowers, leaves, the sprouting and harvesting of rice, the constellations.

Chinese geomancy and all its varied prohibitions also govern lives. The northeast is often harmful, Saturn dangerous; the Good Directions change from one day to the next. In the evening you must orient your bed carefully, and you cannot go anywhere, nor make the smallest decision, without consulting the almanacs. When beginning a voyage, break a small pine branch (for longevity), which assures a happy return, and study the behavior of spiders in the morning for omens about amorous affairs. There is an Imperial Office of Omens, and governments of the most remote provinces are supposed to alert it of anything out of the ordinary. Because an "auspicious cloud" appeared over a northern province, all the prisoners there were released.

The huge gallery of Japanese phantoms has now been assembled, and the night air is swarming with doleful and fearful presences. Cases of possession are numerous, and those who know how to interpret dreams make fortunes. In the Buddhist temples and the Shinto sanctuaries, the daily recitation of incantations, exorcisms, and charms fills the coffers of the clergy. This community of courtiers constantly asks—they ask Buddha, they ask the national *kami,* they use every type of magic—for protection and assistance, often for the most frivolous enterprises.

A tyranny of superstition, together with the many strict demands of etiquette, transforms daily life into an elaborate ballet in which the tiniest misstep disturbs the harmony. But if this artificial world is homogeneous and unified, it is also completely cut off from the other, from the outside, from the real world. It never gets beyond birth and manners. "If one hears a servant say that someone he knows 'is very nice' one cannot help but feel a bit scornful," writes Sei Shonagon. For these ladies, peasants and fishermen at work are—like the white heron—elements in the landscape, which provide them with a verse now and then or sharpen their melancholy, since through all this refinement runs a thread of sadness that they want the bonzes to explain.

And then too, one cries a flood of tears; it's the fashion. In poems, in private journals, it goes without saying that "sleeves are drenched in tears," and even the soldier has a tear in his eye. While they dry them, they write. Much more than they speak. This allows them to cherish their sentiments and, especially, to admire their calligraphy. Calligraphy is the true religion of this aesthetic court, where anyone afflicted with a "bad hand" does not stand a chance of advancement.

You may also observe a slight penchant for the precious and an attraction for young boys. "A willow bud about to burst forth"— that is how a captain of the archers chooses to depict the woman he is courting, by letter, without ever having seen her. The costume of the male—bouffant pants, embossed hat, billowy shirt gathered at the waist—is more dazzling than that of the female, who spends the better part of her life shut in her quarters behind curtains and folding screens. These ladies are less courted and pursued than they would like, as if, with their instinctive good sense, their amazing mastery of the vulgar tongue (they speak Japanese, while the Japanese men often exhaust themselves stammering in Chinese), their sulkiness, their humors, their childbirths, and menstruation, they bring too much reality to the dream sustained by this court.

. . . Across the hedge of lemon trees that separates their residences, the minister of war and his vice-minister exchange poems by courier: an ambiguous, sophisticated banter that the wife of the latter —she is jealous—enters in her journal. They aren't concerned with the campaigns against the Barbarians of the North, and have no interest in going up there to absorb their share of the blows, for along with many other things, they also acquired from the Chinese their distaste for violence and war. These two people are not more militarily inclined than you or I and have simply bought their positions. All power is delegated or occult, but everyone knows that it is entirely in the hands of one great family, the Fujiwara, who for the last four generations have distributed honors, posts, and benefits however they please. The emperor is often no more than a child whom they put in power, or force to abdicate or exile to a monastery; the empress, a very young girl whom they distract with childish games.

The farmers are miserable, but nobody worries about them.

The real military power is very far from the capital, in the fiefdoms of the great and ambitious provincial barons who fence every morning and secretly build up their power.

No one is worried by this threat; they are too preoccupied with an exceptionally melancholy cuckoo that sings at dawn in the garden of the Great Chamberlain of the Left.

Five days from Heian-kyō, on the summit of Mount Koya, the monks who are successors to Saint Kōbō Daishi make elaborate silk paintings, representations of the Buddhist universe. They are called "mandalas." Perhaps these concentric images hold the dazzling cosmic energy and force of attraction that keeps this gracious garden party from going up in smoke, holds it suspended. Few societies have created such a strong impression of drifting on a cloud. People here are too conventional to be cruel. Too worldly to be fervent. Too worried by an etiquette that issues edicts on the length of sabers, the color of robes, the shape of hats . . .

Peace and tranquillity.

In the northeast, the "bad part of the horizon," a temple erected on the flank of a hill protects the city like a fortress against demonic influences. Thus people are sheltered. The courtiers all have the leisure to comment on the last festival as they prepare for the next, and to distribute, buy, and sell offices that don't mean a thing anymore. All the same, sometimes one of them, coming out of a deep reverence, foresees in the faded face in front of him—like a stab in the heart and seven piercing syllables in a poem of thirty-one—the image of his own death.

THE GRAY NOTEBOOK

———————●———————

Kyoto, temple of the Ryōan-ji, April 3, 1964

THREE PORTLY American ladies, solidly encased in hats and corsets and wielding cameras—the type that can digest a few dozen temples, along with a couple of imperial residences, in a single day without even getting a bellyful—go to see the famous Garden of Stones, firmly resolved to gulp it down in one mouthful. The April sun, pale and sly. And the garden (one of the most perfect manifestations of the Zen aesthetic), a few tortured rocks chosen with zealous care by "specialists" some five hundred years ago and marvelously arranged on a dazzling backdrop of white sand. That and no more. Each element of this microcosm has its traditional significance—the sea of clouds, the rocks representing the crane (felicity) and the tortoise (longevity), etc.—as a young official of the Japan Travel Bureau tells the ladies. Explained in a meek voice by this person in a guide's cap, these allegories seem a bit veneered and silly. Faced with her clients' perplexity, she adds that one must not attach too much importance to this symbolism, that the garden is a masterpiece of pure abstraction, an instrument of meditation that allows each viewer to let her spirit float freely.

"Cute little garden," say the three ladies, and the boldest adds in a stentorian voice: "As I look at those rock patterns, I can't help thinking of... Jesus Christ." (!?)

I truly fear, like Kipling, that this West and this East will never meet.

Looking at the way the Japanese visit their own temples, I sometimes wonder if the Japan of today has any better chance of meeting the Japan of the past. Every half hour at the Silver Pavilion

(Ginkaku-ji), entire villages and whole schools press themselves into the bamboo doorway. I tell myself that I have chosen a poor day and should return: ten minutes later, I am alone. Remarkably, that is all it takes to be rid of them...

"Step in a little closer." (And everyone hurries over.) "Built by the order of Lord Yoshimasa, such and such epoch, the two cups of sand on your right represent the repose of the spirit, move along please, we will meet at the number 4 bus stop in ten minutes..."

They take off again in tight groups, aiming their cameras, but many of the photos will be blurred (*Osanaii de kudasaii.* Do not push please!)... because the ones in the back can't help pushing.

Later today, in the lobby of the Kyoto Hotel, I met some other foreigners... these are French. They were cold on the island of Sado. Moreover, after two weeks of cultural circuits and surfeits, they suspect their guides of not having delivered the "soul of Japan."

There are some things you don't say even to the woman you love, or to a beloved brother. And these women, who are not stupid, these women in knit gloves, who in Paris would hesitate to change their butchers (it's a risk, you never know who you'll be doing business with, the lamb won't be as tender), demand that before they leave, someone should wrap up the "soul of Japan" for them. What do they want? Watch this! Suddenly through a simple mental process, their ignorance should be transformed into knowledge, clear-cut and precise please, so that they can discuss it when they get home. I judge them, but I, too, would sometimes like to find my meal set in front of me, and fast. We come to this thin and frugal country with our greedy metabolisms: the whole West is that way. The golden dishes, the maharajahs, the rubies as big as duck eggs—that is what struck our first explorers, that's what they wanted to see, not the frugality that is truly one of the marks of Asia. This is a poem from the earliest Chinese history:

> *The king of Tchou passing the Kiang*
> *finds an arrowhead berry*
> *it's as red as the sun*

it's as big as a walnut
he plucks it, he eats it . . .

He is the lord of a powerful empire, he certainly has the right to munch on a little something. Frugality is the essence; the rest—the armies of five hundred elephants that end up fleeing in panic when it gets hot—that's only confusion. Alexander's soldiers, who were frugal themselves, weren't fooled by that.

Here, anyone who doesn't serve an apprenticeship to frugality is definitely wasting his time.

GENOA,
THE YEAR 1298

———————●———————

L IKE A CAGED SQUIRREL, the Venetian Marco Polo is pacing
in the room where the Genoese are holding him prisoner. He
is chomping at the bit.

It has been three years since he returned from his fantastic voyage to China, six months since he was captured by the Genoese
fleet on the deck of the *Saint Marc,* which he was commanding,
and six months during which he has been fretting, waiting for his
native city to pay his ransom. It is high because, at the end of the
thirteenth century, a man who knows the way to the land of spices
is literally worth his weight in gold.

After all the danger he has been through in twenty years of
travel, he is furious at having been caught in this quarrel between
Genoa and Venice; compared to the world he has visited, it is like a
dispute between villages over a few hundred kilograms of pepper.

To kill time, he dictates his memoirs to his companion in captiv-
ity, an obscure scribe who records them in Latin. Asia fills his
mind: the superb organization of Cambuluc (Beijing), a capital so
grand that no comparison he makes to anything here will convey
its reality—its ten thousand marble bridges under the January
snow; the favors of the emperor Kublai Khan, grandson of Genghis
Khan; the sable cloaks worn by the ambassadors of the north . . .

Sometimes, out of nostalgia, he embellishes his images a little.
But very little. Thus he writes the *Marvels of the World,* where
Europe will hear mention of Japan for the first time. Polo didn't go
there, he just reported it as hearsay in the second book of his tale.

It is called the island of Zipangu (a corruption of the Chinese Ji-pen-kue). *It is very difficult to reach and from Korea requires many days of sailing on very rough seas.*

Pearls are abundant there and gold is so common that all the temple roofs are covered with it, and the tables of the princes are made of solid gold, quite thick. (This explains a rumor he probably heard from Korean shipowners: in Japan, silver is almost as rare as gold, so that the cost ratio of these two metals is one to three instead of one to ten or fifteen, as on the Continent, and this disproportion allows foreigners to do a profitable trade.)

Like the Chinese, the inhabitants of Zipangu suck in a lot of air through their teeth when they talk.

Their sovereign is no one's vassal and sends no ambassadors to Peking.

Polo even mentions the unfortunate attempt of his master, the emperor Kublai Khan, to invade this island twenty years earlier and explains that his defeat was caused by the disputes between the Mongolian generals in charge of the matter and by the typhoon that threatened to annihilate the Chinese fleet . . .

On this point, as on so many others, one can check the truth of his story.

In fact, this is what happened: one-time master of Mongolia, China, and Korea, the emperor Kublai Khan finds it quite natural that Japan pass to his control. In 1268, he sends a threatening letter to "the king of Japan" to demand that commercial relations be resumed. The Japanese, who find his language insulting, return the letter unanswered.

In 1274, Kublai Khan sends a fleet of several hundred sailboats, equipped with twenty thousand of the best frontline troops the world had yet known, Mongolian archers renowned for their discipline, fitness, power, and drive. During their journey, the armada seizes the islands of Tsushima and Ikishima; then they land on the west coast of Kyūshū. The Japanese meet them on the beaches. At first, the samurai horses are frightened by the huge rolling shields that the aggressors push in front of them to protect their advance, and especially by the primitive rockets the Mongol archers use, so the samurai dismount and fight on foot.

Japan has changed significantly since the graceful age of Heian-kyō; front guards no longer "soak their sleeves with tears." The country is emerging from a century of fierce feudal wars that has transformed it into a military nation more interested in punching and fencing than poetry. Compared with the Mongolians, the Japanese of the thirteenth century were mediocre horsemen and only passable archers, but they were excellent swordsmen, and the long blades that they wield in one or both hands produce mortal wounds, with steel so strong that neither Damascus nor Toledo will ever be able to equal it.

The attack is contained and the Japanese reinforcements from the north have not yet arrived, when a storm sweeps the invading fleet, the survivors of which sail back to Korea.

In 1281, Kublai Khan's soldiers return for another attack. There are more than a hundred thousand of them this time, but the Japanese are dug in along the west coast of Kyūshū, waiting for them. They have spent five years building an unbroken wall.

Every day the Shinto sanctuaries and all the Buddhist temples buzz with prayers for the safety of the country or spells to bring down storms, plagues, defeat, and death on the invaders. Under orders from the regent—who holds the real power—they have taken stock of the country's resources and its beasts of burden and mobilized the whole kit and caboodle of the military caste, who, in this affair, showed an admirable willingness.

Here—from one document among many (this one is cited by Sir George Sansom in *Cultural History of Japan*)—is how the country responds to these orders:

The decree of the twenty-fifth day of this month was received here yesterday with the appropriate respect.

The order calls for a list of men, horses, and arms for a punitive expedition on a foreign country. (It is presented as a way to save "face," but each person knows very well what she is up to.)

*The available resources are as follows: my son Saburo Mitsushige and
my brother-in-law Kobujiro. They hasten to join you, marching day and
night. They await your orders with fear and respect.*

*Signed: the priestess Shina, lady of the hamlet of Kitayama (the Moun-
tain of the North) in Kyūshū.*

For three weeks there were battles on the beaches. At the beginning of the fourth, a providential typhoon tears the boats from
their anchors and destroys the immense Chinese armada and its
troops. A divine wind comes to the rescue of a divine race, whose
pride—you can be certain—will only increase after this.

Today we give typhoons pretty, feminine names (Beryl, Laura,
Cathy . . .), most likely to appease their fury. The Japanese of the
thirteenth century baptize this savior-typhoon the Wind-God
(*kami kaze*), and the suicidal pilots of World War II adopted this
name for their cause after all was lost.

For the next ten years, the Japanese keep their guard up, but the
Chinese will never return. While they wait, the Shinto temples
and especially the powerful Buddhist sects, who have their daggers
drawn, bitterly dispute who deserves credit for causing the divine
wind to blow. But it is finally the members of Nicheren sect—an
ultrareformist, violent, radical sect, which displays an unheard-of
insolence and showers the government with threatening letters
demanding moral reform and the exclusion of all other Buddhist
sects as heretical—who carry off the prize, to the great displeasure
of their rivals.

Marco Polo finishes the *Marvels of the World,* which he has written in good faith. His story swarms with precise details confirmed
by history. When he falls into chimeras, they are the ones he shares
with the Chinese, and he is doing no more than accepting the
popular beliefs. His memories may have turned his head now and
then, he may have been duped, but you must realize that a head
not turned by the spectacle of Yuan China, by the caravan routes,
the South Seas and the court of Tabriz—all of which he had seen
on his trip home—would not be worth the shoulders it rests on.

His book is immediately copied and translated, winning wide

fame. Jealous people and skeptics quickly begin a campaign to ridicule these "fables." Their author ends his life in near anonymity; once dead, he becomes one of the Venetian carnival masks, who, with the nickname Marco Million (he boasted imprudently of having possessed great riches), tells the astonished spectators the most outrageous nonsense. Meanwhile, the *Voyages,* an epic written by his successor and competitor, Jean de Mandeville, a tissue of gross lies—men without heads, "ants searching for gold," and stories naively copied from Strabon—becomes a sort of best-seller of the time, experiencing a fantastic success.

That's life, that's publishing.

Despite this eclipse, until the end of the fifteenth century the *Marvels of the World* remains the source consulted by serious navigators. Notably, Christopher Columbus.

He owned a copy—it still exists—worn by numerous readings and covered with notes in the margins. The island of Zipangu and its gold nags at him. His principal objective was to get there; Zipangu could be reached, since the Earth is round, by sailing west. Having proposed his voyage of discovery to Portugal, France, and England, without success, he offers it to Isabella of Spain: to sail west, find Zipangu, and fill their pockets there; then to reopen trade with China, ancient supplier of the luxuries of the Roman Empire, supplies that Islam has cut off from the West. The queen of Spain, who has just recaptured Granada from the Muslims, puts up her jewelry as security and offers him three caravels and a sealed letter for the "emperor of China."

In August 1492, his fleet leaves the Strait of Gibraltar and, after having sailed for a month, enters the Sargasso Sea with a crew appalled by the fluctuations of the compass. On October 11, the crew regains its courage: they see a mulberry branch full of fresh berries floating on the water. The next day, they perceive faint lights, which they take for land and which are really millions of phosphorescent worms risen to the surface for their nocturnal egg-laying. The next day, real land, which they take for Japan . . . and which is only America, or actually the Bahamas.

There, and later on the coast of Mexico, all the Spanish had to do to gather gold was reach down. So history doesn't say that they were disappointed to find America while searching for Japan.

Today, a good many tourists, having just arrived the day before in the Tokyo of department stores, all-aluminum elevators, neon signs, taxis with televisions, the cleanest and most modern subway in the world, have the vague feeling that someone has played the same trick on them.

THE VATICAN

———————●———————

I N 1453, a bull by Pope Nicholas IV gives all the "navigations of Africa *usque ad Indos*" to the king of Portugal—that is to say, all that he can discover to the east of the Guinea coast, wrest from the infidels of Egypt and Happy Arabia, and convert by will or force to the Christian religion.

Forty years later, in 1493, Pope Alexander VI (Rodrigo Borgia—controversial pontiff, passable politician, and excellent erotic poet, whose works no longer seem to receive the attention they deserve) issues the *Inter Caetera Divina* bull, thereby repartitioning the new lands of the planet between Spain and Portugal. The line of separation passes one hundred marine leagues to the west of the islands of Cape Verde, giving Portugal all that is on this side, and all on the other side to Spain. At the antipodes, this imaginary line cuts through just about the middle of the island of Zipangu, which no one knew enough about then to locate on a map, and transforms its habitants into potential subjects of the Portuguese king, Manuel I, the Fortunate, and Isabella the Catholic, ruler of Spain.

Fortunately for Japanese pride, they knew nothing of the casual way their lot had been decided. Sure of their divine origin, they soon adopt the point of view that once their house is put in order the entire universe will submit to imperial virtue and, as the general count Nogi will write much later, "bathe in the same dew of bliss as the Japanese."

Meanwhile, Emperor Ming of China goes to sleep every night

persuaded that the entire Earth belongs to him by celestial mandate, and the idea of a division would never cross his mind for an instant.

In Europe, alas, they ignore all this benevolent protection and this unlooked-for opportunity to acquire a few rudiments of civility from contact with Chinese culture. But the English and the French, unhappy to be excluded from the partition decreed by Alexander VI, quickly put their lampoonists and scribblers to the task of establishing that nothing in the "Testament of Adam" (Francis I) authorizes these monopolies, that the sea is free, and that the lands discovered there belong to the first occupant.

It is intoxicating to dream of this tight-woven fabric of ignorance and pretensions to hegemony that intertwine, superimpose on one another, and cancel each other out. On the whole, little has changed.

"THERE IS NO MEANS OF COMPARISON TO DESCRIBE THAT THING."

At the beginning of the 16th century, after having skirted around Africa and settled grandly in Goa and Malacca, the Portuguese enter the seas of the Far East—a little out of breath. They don't succeed in interesting the Chinese in their business; thinking they should speak loudly, they have a squadron sunk off Canton and are excluded from the official commerce of the empire for their improper conduct. But with anarchy and pirates, there is nevertheless a way —even for undesirables—to traffic a little, and they catch on.

In the spring of 1543, three Portuguese merchants leave Vietnam on the junk of a Chinese pirate headed for the Cantonese coast. During the entire crossing they argue, noisily and continually. These cries, this turbulence, this drama, it's deadly boring. A Chinese loves to be a pirate, but what he loves above all is tranquillity. He drops off his passengers at the port of Ningpo and runs away. There, a few months later, another pirate, "seized with compassion," brings them aboard and sails for Okinawa with a cargo of stolen silk, which others will steal from him. A September typhoon throws them off their route, carries and drops them after

twenty-three days opposite the little island of Tanegashima, south
of Kyūshū. At the far end of the bay, there's a village, and all its
inhabitants are gathered on the shore, their hands shading their
eyes. The Chinese are not without anxiety, and for the Portuguese,
it is truly the end of the world.

It is the first time that Europeans and Japanese find themselves
face to face. For a long time, this encounter was known only through
The Travels of the Portuguese voyager Mendes Pinto, a great liar and
braggart, who pretended to have been aboard that ship, but who
wasn't there (it's been proven); he simply added this incident,
which he had heard second- or third-hand, to his own adventures.
Better to stick to the verbal report given to the island's governor a
few years later by a bonze, who prepared the necessary documents
and testimonies. (For these, I am indebted to the kindness and
the translation of R. P. Jean-Marie Martin, a great connoisseur of
Kyūshū and archival investigator.)

TANEGASHIMA 1543
(From the brush of the bonze Nampo Bushi)

*The year 12 of the Tembun era, a great boat moored in the cove of Nishi-
mura. Impossible to know where it was from. A hundred men were aboard.
Their faces were different from ours and they did not know our language.
All those who saw them found them strange . . .* (I see one of those spar-
kling sand coves that you find in the south of the country, a blue
sky full of an immense wonderment, and the people of this fishing
village scattered along the beach, unsure what to make of this junk
with its high quarterdeck decorated with demons painted in flashy
colors.)

Among the men, there was a young Chinese by the name of Goho. (Probably the reason he is mentioned is that he is the only one who
knows how to write.) *The mayor of Nishimura, who is literate, talks to
him by tracing Chinese characters in the sand with his cane.*

"The men on this ship are unusual-looking. What country are they from?"

*"They are merchants who belong to the race of the Barbarians of the
South. In general, they know justice and the rules governing relations*

between lords and subjects, but they are completely ignorant of the laws of etiquette. They drink without cups (probably they drink from the bottle), *they eat without chopsticks, and they pick up food with their hands.*

They only know what they like and only do what pleases them. They do not read characters and they do not understand their meaning . . .

They are merchants. They are not dangerous.

The Japanese don't pay much mind to merchants. In theory, Asian societies have never made very much of them, placing them lower on the social ladder than the most humble country bumpkin. Besides, by this time Portuguese traders no longer represent their country's elite and lead soft and corrupt lives in their Indian trading posts. Passing the Cape of Good Hope, they usually threw their spoons and forks overboard to symbolize the fact that from then on they would gather the gold of India with their hands, and eat the same way, or else have their Goanese concubines feed them. Their "table manners" leave much to be desired. But for the Japanese, as soon as they know "the rules of relations between lords and subjects"—well, all right, they will be able to understand one another. For the Chinese translator, who certainly understands their concern—there is a reason they shared Confucius—there is nothing more important than to clear up this crucial point.

The mayor, overwhelmed by the responsibility, politely has the junk towed to the neighboring town, where another priest sets up office as an interpreter. And a real sensation is created by something the "Barbarians of the South" have, something they were reluctant to part with. Guess what:

They carry a thing about three shaku (about a yard) *long. This thing has a hollow interior and is smooth on the outside. It is heavy. The interior is generally open, but the end is sealed. At the end, on the side, there is a hole: it is through this hole that they put the fire. There is no means of comparison to describe this thing . . .*

You've figured it out, I hope: it is not a crucifix, not a missal, not a bottle of hooch—it cannot be anything but a gun. There weren't too many things we exported at that time. So:

Here is how the merchant uses it. He places a marvelous powder inside it, he puts in a small white object (a wad): taking this thing, he holds it against his body, closes an eye, sends fire through the hole, there is nothing he can't hit. When the shot goes off, it produces a light like a flash of lightning and a sound like a clap of thunder. Whoever is hit loses his soul . . . It is truly useful.

What Japanese would resist his desire to possess such a treasure? In any case, Tokitaka, who is governor of the island, can't. He wants to get one. He loses sleep over it.

One day, through an interpreter, he says to the Barbarians:
"It is not that I will make a habit of it, but I would like to learn how to use this object."
And the Barbarian responds: "If you want to know the secret of this thing, I will teach it to you." And he adds: "All it takes is having an honest heart (the bonze writes: "Kokoro wo tadashiku shite") and closing one eye."

The Portuguese probably said: "You have to stand up straight." The Chinese translate: "You must not be a coward, with your heart in your stomach." But the bonze soon finds an edifying moral there, and the governor, enchanted, concludes:

To have an honest heart, that is the great law of our low world. If one does that, one will make no mistake.
He continues: "But you say that it's necessary to close an eye. Why, since closing an eye reduces the distance one can see?"
The Barbarian replies (I abridge): "The purpose of closing one eye is to concentrate your vision on an important point. Think of . . ."

That satisfied Tokitaka, and he answered: "Lao-tzu said, 'When one sees little it becomes clear.' "

Which, actually, means the very opposite . . . but apparently it is impossible to keep the governor from elevating the debate. Finally he pays a huge sum to buy two of these "truly useful objects," which he could have confiscated just as easily, and then practices "morning and night without stopping" and becomes a good shot.

What is most clear is that after changing hands the gun hits its mark better than any ideas. It gets to its destination intact; it works. For the Japanese, this is the essential thing. As for ideas, they are known as servant girls and left to turn inside out like gloves; but not guns, unless fired at oneself.

Having learned to mix his powder, Tokitaka asks his arms factory to make copies of the harquebuses. The butt, the fuse, the barrel—they're easy; but they cannot manage to seal the end. The Portuguese, delighted by the civil welcome they received, come back the next year. To learn the secret of making the gun, a blacksmith by the name of Kimbei delivers his seventeen-year-old daughter, Wakasa, to them.

She returned with them a year later. Kimbei went on board, took her back, and, after a few days, told the merchants that she had gotten sick and that the funeral had already taken place. The Barbarians did not cry over this news and did not appear to put much faith in it . . .

To prostitute his daughter in the higher interest of his lord is, after all, a perfectly natural thing. What counts is to get the recipe, and, dead or alive, Wakasa did it so that the harquebuses can go on multiplying in Kyūshū, then in all of Japan. Thirty, three hundred, three thousand. But they are expensive, and only the great feudal lords can offer guns to their armies, enabling them to subdue the minor lords. At the battle of Kawanakajima, barely twelve years later, the air is already totally black with gunpowder.

So! Now they have been introduced. They were sold a real gun, and paid for it with good gold coin. All in all, quite a success.

Personally, I see this transaction in the little port of a little, lost island as a curtain rising on a drama in which the protagonists don't realize the importance of their roles and play them carelessly. On one hand, there is the governor, full of maxims, so courteous, so determined to be "correct" and of course to keep anything useful from escaping his grasp. On the other hand, the three voluble Portuguese, astounded at the great deal they have made, and most likely very dirty under their lace collars. I feel like yelling at them: "Stand up straight, a little dignity, less bragging"—they declared that Portugal was bigger than China—"and fewer grimaces. And don't blow your garlic breath into the nose of your interlocutor, choose your words well, and make a good impression..." But in the end it doesn't matter; they are no more than puppets, their role is modest. It is the gun that holds center stage, and it is perfection.

KAGOSHIMA. "THESE PEOPLE ARE A DELIGHT."
(Saint Francis Xavier, leaving Japan in 1551)

Let each person cultivate filial piety and loyalty to the lord, keep to his place, be prompt to perform his duty; let the samurais work the fields till dawn, because inaction is demoralizing; let the Norm be respected, etc., and our people will be protected from injustice, and all will be well for the State.

Basically, that is the Confucian Decalogue, which the subjects of the ruler of Satsuma, in the south of Kyūshū, have been asked to obey for a generation. Each morning all able-bodied men perform exercises: they are ruled by the rod. And the author of this strict code, head of the powerful house of Shimazu, who became a bonze so that he might govern more easily, does not put himself above the law: "If one among us is caught in an action that is wrong or inconsiderate, then all of us should condemn it without delay."

All goes well for the Shimazu clan, who keep adding to their land, and it is here, in this "moralized" state, in Kagoshima, in the middle of the sixteenth century, that the first soldier of Christ disembarks to sing them an entirely different song.

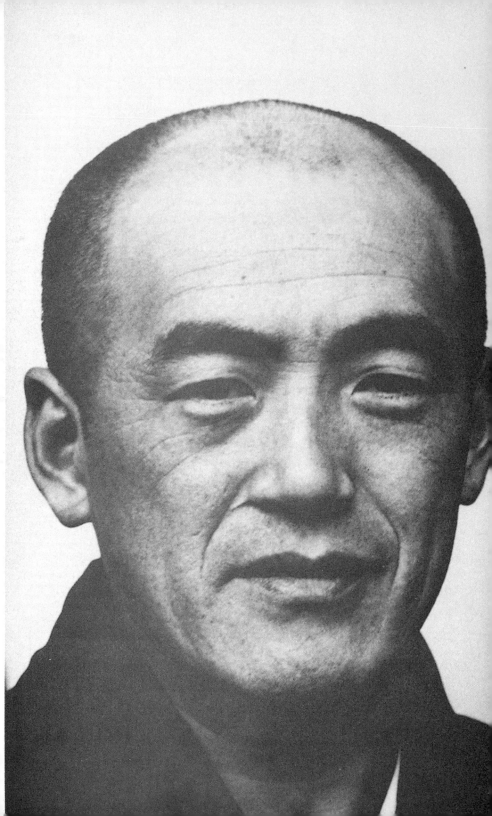

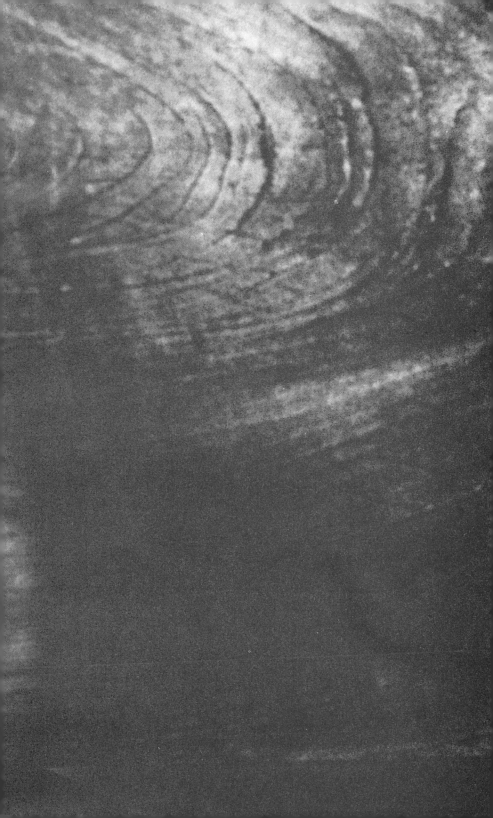

Saint Francis Xavier is the son of a Spanish dignitary. A student of theology in Paris, he met Ignatius of Loyola, succumbed to his magnetism, and, with him and a few others, founded the Society of Jesus, whose missions were approved by the pope. He went to Portuguese India as a papal legate for two years, first to the spoiled luxury of Goa, then to the south, where he baptized—"until his arm was numb"—thirty thousand converts from the lower castes (India offers the filthiest and most destitute). Poor devils who accepted this conversion, the Host, the next life, without hemming and hawing, like a bowl of rice fallen from the sky. Among them, there was not a raja, not a sultan, not one person educated or "of a condition" to offer an honorable resistance before submitting. Francis Xavier was disappointed: just like counting sheep! In one of his letters, he complains that his ministry has been outdone by the Franciscans, who preached everywhere that Christ would have lived among the pariahs, while he is killing himself to explain that Christ would have chosen the Brahmans.

It is in India that he first heard talk of the newly discovered Japanese: the courtesy of their welcome, their correctness, their mastery of themselves. Through these still-vague stories, he sees a system, a power, an adversary worthy of him. And he dreams of making them virtuous, these people "lost in gentility," of making them the citadel of his Church of the Orient.

On the fifteenth of August, 1549, he arrives in Japan, not knowing that Christ had preceded him by three centuries. Actually, the Chinese Buddhists of the Middle Ages had heard about this "Sage" of the West and had transformed him into a bodhisattva who came to Japan under the name of Inro Bosatsu and drowned with his message and his origin in the vast national pantheon.

At the same time, Christendom, having got wind of the virtues of Sakyamuni, claims him under the name of Saint Josephat (a corruption of Bodhisat), and adds him, with his converter, Saint Balaam, to the calendar of saints (November 27) where he gets lost in the crowd just about as fast. But both sides have forgotten this exchange of politeness.

Everything will start over.

Resolved to aim for the top, Francis Xavier asks for an audience with the daimyō of Satsuma, who welcomes him warmly. His black cassock, his natural bearing is a marvel. He wants to preach virtue? Good! Many of the bonzes already do this in the streets: no objection. The example of sages has never been a public problem; the Japanese are tolerant and curious by nature, and all doctrines are good and can coexist peacefully as long as they don't alienate the daimyō's subjects from work and moderation. Finally, central power is weak and leaves elbow room for the lords of Kyūshū; the Portuguese boats that land in their ports bring enormous benefits. Not to mention the famous muskets that give so much pleasure.

A good beginning.

But Francis Xavier still is blind to the art of compromise, that flexibility so often attributed to his order; for the most part, compromise is a lesson of the Orient, and the Jesuits bravely struggle to learn it. He is in the home of the pagan, after all. There is a smell of idolatry everywhere. Bewildered by a society where he comprehends neither the strong or the weak, he plays his part alone, stands out, embarrasses, offends everyone; his mistakes accumulate. When the Zen bonzes who welcomed him as a friend hear him declare that the *satori* (illuminations) of their illustrious Chinese precursors were stuff and nonsense, they expel him from their temples.

When the daimyō of Satsuma learns what the foreign doctor says about the ancestors—who must be venerated—that they are burning in hell because they weren't baptized, he raises his eyebrows and asks him to go preach somewhere else.

When a neighboring lord, who receives the outcast with open arms—counting on buying cannon powder from him—hears him assert that sodomy puts man below the pigs, the daimyō, who permits this pastime (then widespread in the military), turns pale and shows him the door. The scholars who courteously invite him to expound his doctrine do not hide their amusement at his peculiar thesis: a single, perfectly good God creating a very powerful devil to torment the creatures He loves. When he finally tries to convey the rudiments of the Christian doctrine, with the help of inadequate interpreters, in one of the most difficult languages in the world, he translates God as *kami* (an ambiguous term), sin as *tsumi* ("pollution," without moral connotations), and for the rest he uses Buddhist terminology and gets himself into such a maze of mistakes that he is unable to find his way out.

It is a delicate task to bring a new morality to these people who have for so long carefully chosen only what fits them.

Not yet beaten, he visits still more "kingdoms" of Kyūshū, traveling to the capital (Kyoto), where he is received well enough, despite his anathemas. But finally, his heart broken, he leaves Japan in 1551, after converting no more than a handful of plebeians (but who converted with a fervor he hadn't seen in India) and (after Sir George Sansom) only one important lord, who had syphilis and had welcomed baptism.

Beneath this appearance of failure, his mission is a success. Because the Japanese are more sensitive to tone than to abstraction, and the "strangeness" of the doctrine is less important to them than is the character and courage of the man. Moreover, because the breakup of central power is creating a vacuum to be filled by those from the outside. Because above the heads of helpless missionaries, the Japanese lords perceive not halos but a pile of much-coveted harquebuses. Because, finally, Japan just broke relations with China, and in the future only Portuguese vessels will bring the Chinese silks of which the courtesans of Kyoto are so fond.

As for Francis Xavier, despite the resistance that he encountered there, Japan has captured his heart. He is mystified and seduced. This militant man is attracted by difficult countries, by a slightly melancholic moral rigor that he can sense without formulating, by the austere beauty of some of the temples of Kyoto where he has been received—some undefinable quality, born of a tradition of which the West is ignorant and which his Western vocabulary cannot define.

Of all the peoples yet discovered, this is without doubt the best . . . It is just about all that he can say. He leaves behind two priests and asks the Society to delegate some others—the last of the last—for conversions of the elite. They will send them.

It is the beginning of a strange adventure founded on enthusiasm, opportunism, good faith, and misunderstandings. To use a term dear to the Japanese today, you can call it the *Kiristan Boom.*

1582–1592: A MISSION

Kyūshū, Macao, Cochin, Goa, Lisbon, Madrid, Rome... and return.

God is knocking idolatry to the ground in the Indies and bringing new men under his yoke, men who were unknown to our ancestors . . . being the image of the new world (discovered recently and taken first for the coast of Asia), *a world so vast it outweighs the loss of our old world horizons . . .* (a Catholic pamphleteer upon the visit of some Japanese ambassadors to Liège).

After the departure of Xavier comes the golden age for the Portuguese Jesuits. Japan welcomes them. They begin a furious spate of baptisms, no longer just the small fry of the previous period. The great of Kyūshū convert, out of true conviction, curiosity, or interest in the cargo from Macao. And one can see the names Martin Berthelemy, Pie, Gregory, Gervais, Protais, not to mention Ignatius, sprouting up in their genealogies. Since they are good Confucians, their subjects follow, and sometimes there is such an excess of zeal that the Buddhist monks have no choice but to take to the woods.

To the north, in Honshū, a captain named Oda Nobunaga, lowborn but tremendously talented, is in the process of unifying Japan under his control, through his military genius, his grand schemes, and such a use of treachery that it would make Machiavelli blanch. He is made regent, and he prepares to break the backs of the military priesthoods of the Tendai and Ikko sects, who fought his ascension and whose quarrels are a continual source of disorder. He too favors the Christians and the trade they bring.

Among these warring interests are some excellent Jesuits who profit from this routing of Buddhism. They have learned the language, write it a little, mastered the etiquette, and know how to show a "poker face" and navigate with the wind without yielding too much that is essential. Nobunaga, who appreciates their knowledge, goes so far as to invite them to dinner and pepper them with questions on cartography, ballistics, and naval architecture. Now and again, these good rhetoricians still preach in the streets, arousing controversy when they don't get too much opposition from their Buddhist adversaries but packing their bags when they see a Zen monk appear, one of the kind whose questions are so ludicrous and treacherous that they leave even the best theologian *a quia*.

What else could they need? Money, money, money, and a monopoly on this immense parish that the Spanish Franciscans of the Philippines (more detestable than the "gentiles") were trying to get their hands on.

With these goals in mind, Father Valignano, successor to Xavier, sends a delegation of four Japanese Christians, favored with looks and good birth, to visit the pope and Philip II. He chooses them young, fourteen or fifteen years old, so they can better endure the hardships of the voyage, be more affected by the spectacle that greets them, and continue to bear witness to the marvels they have seen for a long time. And to make these emissaries (four children, with a Portuguese priest as nurse and a Chinese servant) seem more prestigious, has them introduced in Europe as "sons of the kings of Kyūshū."

In the spring of 1582, the ship leaves the coast of Japan. The mothers, sure they will never see their progeny again, shed a few tears. Here and there, bells sound. There are one hundred and fifty churches in Japan and over two hundred thousand converts from all ranks: from the miserable peasants of the southwest, who can hardly wait for the promised Paradise after death, to the "King of Bungo," a Christian so fanatical that he organizes shooting parties to track down the bonzes on their lands, hunting them like game.

During the ten years of the trip there and back, the first Japanese to visit Europe keep a journal that the Jesuits will later hold up as a sort of "moral dialogue." Thus, we know what strikes the visitors and how they pass their time. En route, these children discover a passion that Japan will cling to more fervently than their devotion to Christ: Western music.

In Macao, during nine months of waiting, they learn Latin . . . and play the harpsichord, which seems to delight them. At Cochin and Goa, where they are given a generous welcome, more Latin . . . and the lute, the oboe, the spinet. During the interminable trip around Africa, they try to catch flying fish . . . and study counterpoint and harmony, which they claim is already "greatly appreciated by the Japanese." In Evora, the archbishop holds a celebration in their honor, serving a high mass whose polyphonic accents must have pricked their ears.

In Rome, in samurai robes and blunt swords, they stride through a crowd of people to an audience with Gregory VIII, who greets them, bursting with affection, and has four strawberry-pink doublets cut to their size so that no one will laugh at them.

In the midst of this pomp and circumstance, these child-diplomats preserve an impassivity that dumbfounds the Italians. But even if they keep their heads straight, they have lively eyes: few things escape them, and when the slyest of the Venetian magistrates interrogates them in Latin on the sea routes they used, kept secret by the Portuguese, they are quick to sniff out the trap, and no one can get a word out of them. They are led from masterpiece to masterpiece; Tintoretto starts their portrait; but neither the "great painting" nor the marble architecture of the palaces and domes impresses them much. Like good Japanese, they look and memorize—the methods, the tools, the techniques: in short, everything that will be useful to take back with them. On their triumphal tour of Italy, what intrigues them the most, after the lute maker's workshop, is the tour of the glass studios of Murano, and a secret lock that the duchess of Florence works before them many times because they like it so much.

For two years all of Europe talks about the "kings from the Orient." The Counter Reformation takes advantage of these parishioners from the antipodes with their impressive seriousness, and the Huguenots are upset that such good pupils have not come to their domain to look for "the true light."

In 1592, the ambassadors—they are now men—return to Kyūshū, carrying great blessings. Valignano has obtained a papal brief that disposes of the rival Franciscans . . . but it's too late, since the first edict against Christianity is already five years old, and his brand-new bishop's palace has no more than a generation to survive.

Among their baggage, Miguel Seimon, Martin Hara, Mancio Iti, and Julien Nakaura also bring back—there's no doubt about it—a few musical scores, some musical instruments. And unknowingly plant the seeds of *karasiku* (classical music)—this religion that still reigns supreme today in the Japan of "hi-fi" and "coffee-music," where it costs only 20 yen to hear a performance of the *Symphonie Pathétique,* and where the prophets, from Blessed Palestrina to Saint Beethoven, have gone straight into the august Japanese pantheon, without any fuss.

But it is a peculiarity of these long voyages that the travelers bring back everything but what they went to find.

SHIMABARA, 1638

Things are not going well. Things couldn't have gone well. The Jesuits and the Japanese were in love without understanding each other.

Oda Nobunaga's successor is named Hideyoshi. He's a commoner, a great captain, rather high-minded. He sees the value of foreign trade, appreciates the character of the Portuguese priests, invites them to incredible "parties" that raise the eyebrows of all the "people of taste" in Kyoto, and when he is not too drunk, he pumps them for pertinent information. But he also sees the Spanish in Manila and the Portuguese in Macao, he sees their cannons and high-prowed vessels. He sees the Jesuits of Japan participating in many local intrigues, keeping the profits of Western trade away from converted daimyōs, and he sees Kyūshū a step away from becoming a "Christian kingdom." The Franciscans are finally managing to get a foothold in the country, criticizing the work of their forerunners and making the same embarrassing mistakes that their predecessors have finally stopped making. Not to mention the Japanese delegation that went "to pay tribute to Rome," something that made a terrible impression at home.

"Let a stranger in, and he will drive you out of your own home," says a proverb, and Hideyoshi is beginning to see the truth in it.

So he takes action.

His first edict gives the missionaries twenty days to leave the country, under penalty of death, and specifies that the trading ships are welcome as always. But it is not enforced: it's a warning shot, a request for the priests to be more discreet. The Church in Japan does not accept this and redoubles its efforts and its trouble-making. In 1597, a second warning: twenty foreign priests and Japanese disciples are crucified at Nagasaki as an example.

For about twenty years, the edicts of prohibition multiply without effect; the Church continues to grow and the new Japanese converts join the line waiting for martyrdom. Hideyoshi and his successors look but never find a modus vivendi with the Jesuits, and they coexist in complete ambiguity. Thus, to refill their treasury, the priests charge for their service in the Chinese silk trade, and they are so shrewd that Hideyoshi begs many of the offenders, whom he had prohibited from traveling, "to speculate" on his account. They paid up... but now and again their flocks pay with their lives, and each martyr is worth ten new converts.

The Dutch arrival in the Far East in the midst of the seventeenth century deprived the Jesuits of one of their best cards. The merchants of the Oost Indische Companiie were eager to do business without holy water. From then on, the Japanese can play the *Komojin* (red-skinned Dutch) against the *Nambanjin* (Barbarians of the South).

In fifteen years of massive persecutions, Japanese Christianity was destroyed. The choice is to either renounce God or die on the cross, in boiling oil, in the lava of the Kyūshū volcanoes... and the Japanese choose to go with a willingness, a courage, a contempt for this low world that astounds and edifies the West. In the Japanese ethic, it is expected that you die for your master: even a scoundrel knows that rule. And there is even more reason for it when the master has already died for you. In the eyes of the Japanese converts, Christ had become the supreme daimyō, and all the many "obligations" society imposes were transferred to him and his advantage. To be a martyr is to do a small part of your duty. There are hardly any apostates, who could be made to renounce "the Father, the Son, the Holy Ghost, the Mother of God and all the angels . . . "—that is, by the entreaty they had placed above everything else, forgetful of the "general Good."

It is on the Shimabara peninsula, in 1637, that the last act is played out. There, the Christians join forces with the starving peasants (thirty thousand in all), and led by four baptized samurai, they seize a rice depot and a fortress, where they hold off a two-month siege by an immense, trained army. When the fortress falls, all the survivors (men, women, and children) are massacred. It was the cannons of a warship, obligingly loaned by the Oost Indische Companiie, that first breached the castle walls, taking the money owed for the Spanish terror in Flanders out on the backs of foreigners and natives.

That same year an imperial edict declared: *No Japanese ship whatsoever is authorized to leave the country, and anyone who disobeys this order will die. All Japanese returning from foreign lands will also be put to death.*

Ships from the high seas are prohibited from docking, and lookouts are placed on the hills of Kyūshū to warn of possible sails in the distance.

It's over. There are no more foreigners in Japan, except for a small Chinese community on Nagasaki, and a handful of Dutch merchants under strict surveillance, abandoned like lepers on an islet in the bay where they account for an immensely profitable trade with Canton, India, and Amsterdam.

But it is hard to close a port that has been wide open, and once in a while in Nagasaki, a Japanese with enough curiosity about science manages to acquire one of the Western books that Chinese sailors smuggle in at the risk of their lives. Sometimes hidden between an astrology book and a treatise on anatomy, the port authorities find and seize a small Chinese catechism by the Jesuits of Beijing. Seller and buyer are then hanged . . . or crucified, since the authorities who have attempted to eliminate this dangerous doctrine have unintentionally preserved its symbol and added this practice—which they judge practical, expedient, and above all exemplary—to an already well-stocked arsenal of tortures.

In the next two centuries, Japan—which Europe has loved so

quickly and known so poorly, little more than politeness, porce-
lain, and martyrs—is almost entirely erased from the Western
imagination.

Take the literature of the eighteenth century: it swarms with
Hurons, Incas, Hottentots, Persians, the Chinese, the Mameluks,
"wise Orientals," and "Good Savages"; with theories—firecrackers
that the philosophers slide under the thrones of kings or under the
Episcopal pulpit. You find everything there, even Confucius, the
"Chinese Socrates." But not one Japanese.

At this time, entrenched behind its edicts, its belt of typhoons
and waves, the Japan of Tokugawa meditates on the failure of a
business that had begun so well, and transforms the foreigner into
a scapegoat or a scarecrow, and swears that he will never be allowed
to return.

THE GRAY NOTEBOOK

———————●———————

A S I WALKED back home, I was suddenly filled with an inexplicable gaiety by the sight of a huge, black fly cleaning himself on a dazzling pyramid of fresh eggs in the grocery store. I felt as if I had just hatched from an egg myself. I went to drink sake at the home of two Koreans who keep a bar as big as a Norman buffet, between the Shimogamo steps and the elder trees in the little cemetery. Mother and daughter: Sioux faces, matte skin stretched taut across strong cheeks, obsidian eyes, bold and gay, superb teeth. Both of them look like magicians or reincarnated foxes. This morning, my head a little sore but my spirit bright, I have shed my old skin somewhere in the expanse of sleep. The new skin is still tender and painful, but I know that I will find a way to be comfortable living in it here for a few years; the other really will not do anymore. On the breakfast table, I found a watercolor, still wet, of three persimmons; Eliane has taken up painting again. An excellent sign. As I hoped she would in this country I love so much. Rain is pouring down on the new leaves; the light changes every instant. The sky is like a luminous sponge that a huge hand squeezes and releases. Tonight, I saw all of the events of Japanese history in a dream, lined up like a series of images from popular culture, in acid colors, here and there a close-up of a bit player, of a sorrowful or stupefied face. A little like a child looking at a magic lantern.

KYOTO, APRIL 1964

(at a Noh spectacle of the Kongo school)

The room is small, somber, with a patina like a cooking pot, the matted floors gleaming in the half-light. The public: old men and women, heads bent, coils of hair pulled over shiny baldness. Faces of women full of mischief, wrinkles, and serenity. The men, with a duller air, very scholarly, a little moth-eaten. All murmur in low voices and follow the program that they hold open on their knees. This hum responds to the actors, accompanies them, and links the scene to the room in the same way that the "response" links the Catholic priest with his flock. Here, no stiffness, no constraint: at any moment the spectators may leave their places, tiptoeing toward the exit in their linen socks in order not to disturb anyone, get some air, a cup of tea, smoke, then return just as carefully in order not to miss an especially awaited or appreciated line or speech.

. . . A chestnut popping on the coals, a furious cricket singing in flour. Is this music? Listening to the music of Noh for the first time, I asked myself this question. In addition to the chorus of narrators, a flute and two drums—each shaped like an hourglass—make up the entire orchestra. When the libretto requires it, they add a larger drum. These two drum players, their instruments balanced on a shoulder or a knee, must be seen to be imagined: with great effort, the right hand pulls away from the drumskin, the fingers tense; the Adam's apple moves up and down; the whole attitude suggests an intolerable tension which is relieved by a feeble groan. Then the hand falls again, but it doesn't tap at every beat, and when it does tap, it does so gently, with fingers of wool. "Nothing in excess," wrote Zeami, who was one of the founders of Noh in the fifteenth century. Sometimes an almost animalistic cry —a kind of strangled "yooup!"—precedes the sound of the drum. But this incongruous mixture does not make one laugh. What is most astonishing is that these musicians with their tortured expressions; these immobile narrators, their fingers pressed to their fan, who deliver in bursts a text that I don't understand; this music so slow, so wrenchingly painful, possess such an incantatory power, a magic so complete that the foreign listener, barely containing his amazement, is truly "carried away," taken by something stronger than himself into the nocturnal and rarified space of Noh.

And I had not expected to like it either: some "connoisseurs," and esoteric bores, had spoiled my pleasure in advance by assuring me, that, ignorant as I was, I would not get anything from the spectacle. (Have you ever drunk a good bottle of wine with a connoisseur? It is a form of torture.) Thus forewarned and on the defensive, within half an hour I was carried away by the quality that I had least expected from this theater: the power.

This is what Paul Claudel wrote fifty years ago: "In tragedy something happens, in Noh someone appears." This someone arrives on stage down a passage visible from the room. He is called the *Shite,* he plays the god of hell, a bodhisattva, a demon, a soul in pain, etc. He wears a mask, often a frightening one; his costume —yards of crisp brocade—has an indescribable and sinister elegance. This character, whose approach is signaled by a special drum and who advances with nightmare slowness in his white slippers, represents the otherworldliness of Noh. The actor waiting on stage, face uncovered, is a human: a wandering priest, an empress who has taken up religion, a woman searching for someone who has disappeared. This character is the *waki,* who stands on the edge of two worlds, ready to either give or receive a long-awaited peace. His costume—I should say his plumage—is more modest, like that of the female bird of paradise. He explains the story and prepares the audience for the apparition for which he will serve as witness, and for which he may represent deliverance. This wait is highly charged, you are unaware of time passing, and the coming of the *Shite* is a true denouement. Theatrically and spiritually, the Noh unravels. It is a means of liberation.

This first time I began to daydream at times, and I took a few breaks to stretch my legs. Each time I returned to the stage—the demonic, red hair of the *Shite* (in this Noh, a guardian of hell), the chorus with its voices from beyond the grave—I was soon swept along again. "The Noh," Zeami wrote, "is like a night within the heart of the day." Or like the silence of a mouth closed by snow.

NOH THEATER. TOKYO, MAY 1965

Those who practice this noble art live at a distance, obscure and intense like hundred-year-old carp under fifteen fathoms of black water. After having exercised my lungs sufficiently, I finally made a friend in the Noh theater. We wrote each other letters many times before exchanging a glance: in these depths, one must not rush things. He took the initiative by informing me of his age and thus establishing that he was my elder. Seniority is very important here. With that established, everything went very easily. All the more so since he wanted to improve his French, which he spoke infinitely slowly and affectedly. He received me in underwear and long tights in the antechamber where he waits for his guests. A narrow spectral face with deep eyes, long white hands that float around his mouth like algae as he carefully constructs small bits of sentences. He is the seventh generation of an illustrious dynasty of actors from the Kanze school. He was required to take over his father's work, the costumes and masks of the family patrimony, and his son will do the same. He leads me to the wings to introduce me to his successor, who is trying on the costume for the next show. The child is six or seven years old, with a face as smooth as a chestnut, grave and melancholy eyes, already professional. He is kneeling motionless and wearing the magnificent black mane of the demon.

"This is the hair of a funerary steed," says the father, and then: "Is that how you say it?"

"You say mane. Funerary steed is very literary."

"Yes, the mane of a funerary steed."

In Noh, only noble terms are used, and formal language that doesn't exist anywhere else in Japan.

When he is searching for a word, my friend pauses and thinks; this can take fifteen or twenty seconds. It is a good thing I have all the time in the world. When he is in doubt, he asks me: "Simple future of *pouvoir?*"

"*Je pourrai, tu pourras, il pourra.*"

"No! more polite."

"You cannot be more polite."

As if to make up for being only the Great Chamberlain of the Left or the ghost of a famous warrior, the Noh actors, sagging under their marvelous costumes, start by telling you their genealogy and their itinerary: "I am the ghost of... son-in-law of ... from the clan of... coming from... going to, passing by..." And the cold, sad geography of the Japan of the past unfolds for you: Bungo, Echizen, Matsu, Oku, the provinces that they have crossed, the hills, the valleys, through storms and snow. Because of the rhythm of Noh, travel is so slow that winter always overtakes them en route. They travel in tiny steps across a sort of mental Tibet.

A Noh plot: A weary traveler falls asleep near a well; the shade of a woman who threw herself into the well years before comes out of it and performs a dance expressing the unhappy love that drove her to that end. The traveler awakens, inexplicably moved by a dream that—you feel—will steer him toward a spiritual awakening. This can easily hold you spellbound for two hours. I especially like the economy; after all, does a human life really contain more than this action? Everything else is just peripeteia, which they have the good sense not to put on stage.

There's no need to be a great scholar to be moved and ravished by Noh theater. But, two things: be aware that Noh is slower than all that the word "slowness" suggests in the West, and get a translation of the text (texts exist for all the major Noh productions), which is often great poetry. As for the style of masks, the different ways of beating the drum, the various schools, these are erudite garnishes, which add no more to the meal of a hungry person than the name of the dish. On the other hand, an empirical knowledge of Japanese Buddhism, acquired casually—while shuffling in night hospitals; in provincial train stations; in those little country temples where monks sleep over their beer bottles; in short, in all those slightly marginal places that bring to mind everything sad and transitory in this world—this knowledge will add greatly to your pleasure.

PAX TOKUGAWA

———————●———————

A COUNTRY THAT IS hard to reach and that puts itself under quarantine. This is not an isolated case: the Chinese empire also closed itself off, telling the English emissaries in the eighteenth century that it had never had "the slightest need of any products of their country's industry." The Japanese do not have this sort of conceit. They do not isolate themselves out of arrogance but out of caution. At first, their withdrawal, their avowal of weakness, is a great success. The first Tokugawa, or their advisors, are subtle politicians who exploit the morality of their citizens as much as they can.

Scorn pleasure and devote yourself to thankless tasks. This is the first commandment of this new regime, one of the most strictly policed that history has ever known. And it pays. The shogun (temporal ruler) moves his court to Edo (Tokyo) to escape the intrigues of the ancient capital and to keep an eye on the vassals of the North. All the great feudal lords are obliged to leave their families hostage. It is illegal to draw up a map or improve the roads—thus the movement of insurgents is hindered. Japan is full of these barriers, controls, city tolls, familiar to anyone who has seen a Japanese historic film. Coastal and river traffic finds itself growing accordingly, sailor guilds get richer, and the merchants (a scorned race which, by sumptuary edict, is prohibited from carrying silk) hoard, lend to the nobles, and secretly expand their power. The nation is unified and reaps the fruits of peace. But the peasants are cut down as much as they are flattered; they are taught that virtue lies in working harder and eating less. And they obey, paying the price for this precarious equilibrium. There is an immense population of unemployed samurai who don't know what to do with their swords and their time. For better or worse, they are directed toward the domestic arts: tea ceremonies, flower arrangement, the gardening culture, and certainly . . . etiquette.

Formalism, ultraconservatism, codification, thought control, political espionage raised to the level of a fine art . . . and it all works. The entire country functions, the whole land is militarized, organized into hierarchies, down to the bordellos, which have four ranks of courtesans. If the philosophers of the West could have seen this strange machine working, they would have lost sleep over it.

But they don't know about it. During this period there is only one report from a Westerner, the German doctor Kaempfer, who administers emetics, herb teas, and enemas to the merchants of the Oost Indische Companiie stationed on the island of Deshima at the end of the seventeenth century. He records all that he learned there, and his enormous *History of Japan* is still valuable today. The fact is that the best travel books—like those of Polo, Bernier, Tavernier, and Chardin—are often written by people involved in commerce. Buying, selling, and profit are the first words in the international vocabulary, and the merchants' strict observations avoid the silly infatuations that will quickly take over the literature once poets start to travel. With a trader, you don't have to worry about flights of oratory, even less with these stubborn and apoplectic traders from Amsterdam, who let themselves be bled by the barber and lectured to by the minister once a week, who bravely risk their hide on the worst seas of the world, and whose faces obliged Franz Hals to use so much vermilion. As long as they can import Chinese silk and export Japanese copper, they are glad to accept all the harassment—searches, interrogations, isolation—to which the Japanese subject them. Business is business, and the profits are enormous. It's easy enough for Kaempfer to fall into the errors of belief of his time: to take the Buddha for a "Negro impostor from Egypt" and Shintoism for the travesty of an authentic revelation that the Japanese had received at the tower of Babel. But he makes no mistake about the nature of power nor about the unparalleled civic sense that made it work. In his portrait of Japan, he shows his admiration: a self-sustaining island, rich in gold and in silver; excellent products; a disciplined and frugal population that carries cleanliness to the point of fanaticism; omnipresent power; effective police; prompt justice; an always-appropriate alternation between honesty and hypocrisy—in short—the best-governed state in the world. On the whole, he understood it quite well, with one interesting exception: *Examining the field of their knowledge, one discovers that philosophy does not have a place.* He was right. It isn't there. It may never have been. In its place is an adulterated Confucianism that promoted the good of the state and, forced to carry everything, has lost all substance.

No country, even one as frugal as Japan, can live without ideas. In the eighteenth century, stability is succeeded by stasis: a hypocritical and quibbling moralism, a frustrated immobility, exhortations to virtue so vehement that they are unlikely to be followed. With some difficulty, the Japanese convert from rice to money as a standard of exchange, with shifts in value that benefit the usurers and ruin the growers. The peasant, crushed by taxes, has no recourse other than to revolt; he can always find some unemployed samurai to lead one, and leave his skin that no longer has a master. The edicts against foreigners are periodically renewed. Japan maintains a comfortable but largely theoretical xenophobia, since the last "Barbarians" are the Dutch, confined to Deshima, where some intrepid Japanese, eager to acquire an education, secretly search them out. For the Japanese of this era, all knowledge of the outside world is contained in one word, *rankaku* (the science of Holland), and the first things they want to learn are—you guessed it—military surgery and, especially, ballistics. The Rankakujin (Japanese fans of Dutch knowledge) have no confidence in ideas, which can deceive them; they put their faith in their trajectories, which never do. For now, the West's trajectories don't match Japan's: with a few slight exceptions, they know nothing about each other. And when the American captains of Commodore Perry's fleet forced Japan to open up to outside trade, in August 1853, one would have searched in vain for a civilized corner of the planet that was more poorly informed than Japan.

LE TEMPS RETROUVÉ, 1854–1944

———●———

The world is just as the Barbarians made it,
and it forces us to use their weapons.
(A character in *The Three Bamboos,* by Robert Standish)

O N FEBRUARY 11, 1854, black steamships mounted with cannons are seen in Edo bay; and the sabers, the arrogance, and the primitive popguns of the samurai can do nothing against them. Perry had returned for their answer. Along the quays and in the shogun's palace, there is panic, and power is ready to yield.

America forces several Japanese ports to allow entry to its ships and installs a consul in Shimoda. The Russians appear soon after and open three other ports, laying claim to the Kuril islands, although their possession was contested. Then the British; later the French. Only the Dutch, who play fair, offer to pay—a brand-new steam frigate—for the advantages they demand (but these barbarians have known the Japanese for two hundred years).

Six years later, a Japanese delegation goes to the United States to ratify the treaty that nation has imposed on them. The ambassadors are astounded by this crude and energetic El Dorado, where one risks losing face at each step, amazed at the size of the steam liner, *Great Eastern,* and aghast at the tumult of the congressional debates, which they compare in their reports to the cries of the fishmongers at the huge market in Edo. At their first official banquet, they found the presence of flunkeys behind their chairs so insulting (in samurai etiquette, placing a man in back of a guest is a mortal offense) that they consult one another in Japanese to decide if they shouldn't get their swords from the cloakroom and attack these oversized chickens in green-and-gold livery. But there are some situations where honor must wait. The treaty specifies a maximum 5 percent import tax and the right to move residents into the major civil ports, exempt—this is the most humiliating— from Japanese laws. The other powers obtain almost identical terms; Western trade quickly kills an economy that was already sick and fuels a xenophobia that was already smoldering.

In short, the barbarians move in and make themselves at home . . . all because the Japanese did not have coastal batteries, because the people who would have built them were rotting in prison for having read Dutch books, and because there is something rotten in the state of Amaterasu.

Japan sets out to remedy this with a diligence that the West, in all its travels, had never before encountered. In Kyūshū, the great clans are teeming with remarkable men—some familiar with the "sciences of Holland"—who have always considered the shogun a fraud and an upstart. They rise up against him, wallop his army, and restore the forgotten emperor to his place on the throne, and in the popular imagination, and move him to Tokyo. Because they revere this symbol of national greatness, and because they needed this sovereign symbol to galvanize their energies and make acceptable the reforms they are planning. Quick as a flash, all the "retrograde" edicts are abolished, and the fiefdoms of the feudal lords are returned to the Crown. The samurai, deprived of their two swords, make excellent aides to the ministries, the civil service, and budding businesses. In April 1868, the young emperor Mutsuhito, who brought in the Meiji era (enlightened government), announces to his subjects that "for the security of the empire, Knowledge should be searched out everywhere it can be found."

The restoration, begun to the cry of *sonno joi* (honor the emperor and banish the Redheads), actually follows a more realistic program: welcome the Redheads and discover their secrets. To detest the foreigner is one thing . . . but without energy from the last Tokugawa, the Japanese were in a stupor, and so they enroll in his school more or less willingly. And this time, they are in a hurry.

In the daily life, work, and feelings of the Japanese, there is a rhythm made up of alternating periods of rest—a sort of blanket of reveries—and dazzling speed. During the first years of the Meiji period, the Japanese accelerate: 1869—agrarian reforms are established, and the first telegraph set starts to hum; 1870—the first lighthouses, built by the Englishman Brunton, begin their operation on the coasts; 1871—the first Western-style court of law, and an army of draftees train "French-style"; 1872—a naval arsenal, the Tokyo-Yokohama railroad, a postal service, and obligatory education . . .

Not without problems, certainly. The peasants, for example, don't want anything to do with the ways of the Barbarians, so often held up as bogeymen. Now, suddenly, they are told to convert to their ways. The installation of an electric cable seems like sinister "Christian magic" to them, and they fear it will be accompanied by human sacrifice . . . so they revolt. When the *eta* (a group of outcasts) are promised "citizenship," the rural peasants of the north, who find themselves deprived of "inferiors," lose their heads and rise up. They are told: "His Imperial Majesty wants it this way . . ." When that doesn't work, the troops, who need practice, are sent in, and the reforms go through.

All of this, all entirely new, is accomplished in less than five years! It is the response to Perry's cannons. It is also the first time that a country in Asia has taken up the gauntlet.

Asakusa, in northern Tokyo, is one of those pleasure quarters that only the big cities of the Far East possess. Paper lanterns, archery, acrobats and astrologers, vendors selling fried dough, aphrodisiacs, sugar-candy suckers stuck on bamboo skewers, public calligraphers, streetside storytellers who use a wooden phallus to accent their tales, rows of brothels . . . Around 1875, a person could go there and get a glimpse of the "outside world" by looking through the lens of a sort of kinetoscope and excitedly moving the pedal that makes the picture change. There are many of these machines, they cost no more than a *sen* (the price of a bowl of rice), and they create a sensation. Here, from a chronicler of the period, are the images that unfold:

A steel bridge in London that is longer than a rainbow. A palace in Paris (?), higher than the clouds. A furious Russian general pulling a soldier's

*mustache. An Italian woman resting with her arm around her dog. An
escaped balloon floating in the sky. At the last machine, one can see the
Goddess of Beauty lying nude on her bed: her skin a brilliant white, except
for the beauty mark below her navel. Unfortunately, one of her legs, bent,
hides the most interesting . . .*

If for a *sen* more you could look into the mind of the spectator—
who might already have traded his paper parasol for an umbrella
with stays—you would find in the middle of a dizzying carousel
of incredible "novelties," wonderful mechanics and "Western-
style" notions, an obsession that the whole country shared: to "pass
the test of the West" and correct these humiliating treaties.
They're ready to buy the necessary equipment: a little Darwin, a
little Adam Smith, a bit of the rights of man, and a few American
preachers, if you insist . . . and if it is necessary to dress up as a
European to get a diploma, that won't stop them! Too bad if the
frocked coat is too long, the cut not very becoming, the hard collar
awful, and the shoes uncomfortable (especially after the mazurka).
And too bad if the new ideas fit as poorly as the clothes. A cool
head will be able to make these minor adjustments. What they
mainly need are machines that can be bought with tea and raw
silk, since it is thanks to their machines that the barbarians have
been able to dictate their terms here.

Instead of counting to ten while bouncing a ball, the young girls
of the Meiji era sing a nursery rhyme, still well known today, that
proves the Japanese well disposed toward technology: ". . . gaslamp,
steam engine, lightning conductor (the Japanese are terrified of
thunderstorms), telegraph . . ." They do not sing "Jesus, Spinoza,
Goethe, Lincoln, Voltaire . . ." And if they *were* more literary, they
would sing names that wouldn't mean a thing to us, because the
requirements are not so vigorous in the cultural realm; they translate whatever falls into their hands, and the first "bestsellers" are
manuals of domestic tasks and mediocre Victorian novels that they
like because they praise virtue. Then, among many other authors,
Rousseau, because he says that nature is good; Turgenev, because
his melancholy sounds familiar to them; and finally Jules Verne,

because the Japanese don't do things halfway and if they have to think "modern," they might as well think futuristic.

While Japan is so taken with Europe, Europeans are not too interested in Japan . . . except for the French Impressionists, who fall in love with the labels on cases of tea imported from Yokohama. These are very ordinary illustrations (which we find rather beautiful) to which the Japanese pay not the slightest attention. Add to this some aging "fan cases" and some badly colored prints that are soon the rage in Europe. And that's the route—a decadent, pale, and sickly aestheticism—used by Japan, so concerned with technique, to finally move into the long-vacant place in the mental geography of the West—*after* the Klondike gold rush and Buffalo Bill's prairie.

From the arsenal of Western concepts, the Japanese are quick to seize on this one: those who have gunboats can "carry progress to those who don't." In 1876, they send their first boats to Korea to imitate "Commodore Perry's coup" and impose a treaty that follows, to a tee, the one they were forced to sign. In 1894, in an explosion of national shame, they finally manage to revise their own treaty. That same year, they attack China and beat them hands down on land and at sea; they seize territory until Germany, France, and of course Russia, which has the exact same designs, force them to surrender in the "interest of world peace." These events demonstrate a remarkable hypocrisy, a perfect formula for the Japanese, who take it up for their own advantage. But a country can't attack the whole world at once, and Japan pays the price for this failed rebellion. At the same time, the 230 million tael in reparations paid by the Chinese give new life to the economy and enable the Japanese to purchase new armaments.

"Do what you like with China, but hands off Korea." Basically, this is what young Japanese diplomacy tries to make Russia's immense empire understand. In vain. The Russians fortify Port Arthur at the end of the Liaotung peninsula, where they maintain a squadron; they fortify Vladivostok; are practically the masters of Manchuria; and push their forest exploitation up to the Yalu River. Japan silently prepares for war, with the care it devotes to important

business—buying the latest brand of American explosives, install-
ing the latest radio in its ships, and memorizing the works of its
future adversary, Admiral Makarov, after they are translated by
Admiral Togo (of whom the Russians had never heard).

FEBRUARY 1904, BEFORE PORT ARTHUR

The Yellow Sea is foggy. A ship can lie at anchor a few cable lengths
off the coast without attracting attention. On the fifth of February,
a Korean spy swims away from the fortress and rejoins a Japanese
trawler, having learned that a reception will be given for the wife
of the Russian admiral on the night of the eighth. The officers will
be on land—and probably drunk after toasting their emperor. That
night, a squadron of Japanese torpedo boats attacks, destroying
three frontline ships. War is declared the next day. In the weeks that
follow, Japanese troops landing in Korea besiege the citadel. The
taking of Port Arthur is a heroic slaughter foreshadowing Verdun:
one hundred thousand dead in a twenty-five-mile area, fifty-eight
thousand of whom were Japanese. Russians and Japanese show
great courage going to their deaths: one side wearing icons around
their necks, the other carrying boxes for sending their ashes home,
boxes that already bear their "posthumous names." On this heap
of cadavers, the victorious general, Nogi, and General Stoessel, the
vanquished, exchange white horses, a beautiful gesture that the
Western press, who has been following the match, "blather about"
until they run out of steam.

The Russian ogre . . . David and Goliath . . . the Prussians of Asia
. . . the *bushidō* (the military virtues: a term the Japanese start to
use to define their national mystique, a fake tradition without any
well-defined ethical content) . . . Admiral Togo: an inscrutable
hero, charismatic and mysterious. He acts like a competent sailor,
courageous, modest almost to the point of self-effacement—just a
cog in the machine, who says modestly after his victory, "Any one
of my colleagues would have done the same."

While one continues to spout a lot of hot air and stomach-turning clichés, and to pull the wool over one's eyes, the war's last act is played out in the straits of Tsushima. There, in the spring of 1905, Togo intercepts and destroys a Russian fleet that had sailed from the Baltic and, after a miserable odyssey around Africa, arrives exhausted and too late to come to the aid of Port Arthur. A phantom squadron: an old battleship patched up a bit and filled to the brim with bad coal from Cardiff; "modern" cruisers so well greased with bribes that they go from one breakdown to the next; crews of peasant/seamen devoured by malaria and homesickness; and cannons that the priests sprinkle with holy water each day. Not only that, but the Russian second division is commanded by a dead man: Falkersam, the rear admiral, has just succumbed to a fever and now lies, cast in cement, in an open coffin between two pairs of candles. For the Japanese, the spirit of a dead enemy is more terrifying than a living one. If the Russians had understood their enemy, they would have broadcast this story on the radio, "Death ship commanded by a ghost" . . . they keep it absolutely secret. Instead, they paint their hulls black to "frighten the Japanese," but this color doesn't scare them; it helps their artillerymen hit their target.

For thirty-six hours, these two worlds that do not understand one another exchange shells, and score bull's-eyes from carefully calculated parabolas. And on the evening of May 27, you can see sailors—Russian and Japanese—in the cold waters of Tsushima clinging to the same spars, brother-victims of mathematics.

"AS LONG AS THERE ARE NEW WORLDS TO CONQUER, THE JAPANESE SAMURAI WILL SEIZE THEM."

(from the newspaper Nichi-nichi*)*

If Europe had read the Japanese dailies after the victory, it would have found numerous proclamations in this style and would perhaps have perceived that the "new David" had a healthy appetite too. But they went unread.

Japan, however, followed the European press attentively as it

commented on the smallest Japanese acts. Japan knew the importance of this test; in fact, in the eyes of the West, it had passed its
final exam: that of "good conduct." The Japanese troops in Manchuria and in their battle against Port Arthur are absolutely
exemplary: the wounded Russians are cared for admirably, the prisoners treated humanely and fed better than the Nipponese infan-
try. Not a single case of brutality or pillage. This makes Europe
blush, since its forces, some years before, had foolishly sacked the
forbidden city of Beijing.

It all showed in this attitude: the respect inspired by those
Russian muzhiks, who fight like devils, the high moral quality of
the Japanese military staff... and also, the fact that they want to
"pass with flying colors." (Because they were occupying Korea at
the same time, and there, with no jury to impress, they didn't use
kid gloves!)

An excellent impression—even the Red Cross praises them. The
Japanese student passes *maxima cum laude*. He is patted on the
shoulder. Then, for a second time, Europe arranges to deprive Japan
of the fruits of its victory and to obtain a "good peace" treaty for Russia, one that doesn't provide for a kopeck of payment to the victor.

Japan, sucked dry, ruined by its effort, lacks the strength to
overthrow its government, and the emperor calms the people with
this phrase (which later becomes historic, when it is reissued after
Hiroshima): "We must accept the unacceptable and support the
insupportable."

And they do support it, but to this day, they are completely convinced that no foreigner can understand their country's virtue and
that, outside of Japan, good manners do not pay.

The rest of the story is better known. In 1914 Japan declares a
war on Germany that distance saves them from waging, doubles its
tonnage, and increases its reserve in gold sixfold by selling arms
and munitions to the Allies. In 1923, Tokyo is flourishing—it is
the biggest city in the world—when an earthquake, and the fires
it triggers (it is September and the *hibachis* are already burning to
heat the wood houses) destroys the city from top to bottom. One
hundred thousand dead, plus a few thousand scapegoats—Koreans

or Japanese Communists—who "lose their skins," as the stricken population explodes in a sort of hysterical rampage.

With the thirties come exciting but somber events, which the Japanese had to suffer: the occupation of Manchuria; the assassination of liberal politicians and generals from the old school; the purge of the universities; expansion of the industrial empires of the firms Mitsui, Mitsubishi, Sumitomo, etc., which means fast machines replaced cheap labor; new markets; conquests... The mikadoism (imperial Shintoism) profits indirectly from a military that doesn't honor those who took Port Arthur... A tyrannical xenophobia and a military police (*kempeitai*) better than the Bolshevik *Guepeou*... Finally, the long Chinese war, with fighting as ferocious as the Russian fighting had been clean.

In the West, the image of Japan begins to darken. The Western attitude went from the swoons of Pierre Loti to a veiled antipathy. Japanese bicycles for ten francs, pounds of watches, cultured pearls by the bushel—the term "Japanese junk" is not coined for nothing. At first it was flattering to see such a different people convert so eagerly to Western techniques; but when the imitation becomes good enough to menace our markets, there is grumbling. Sour talk of cheap goods, disloyal competition, "dumping," and the "yellow peril" come back into style. This efficient but closed nation inspires mistrust, and the West responds by ridiculing it: their reverences; their eternal smiles; their gauche adaptation of Western style— those suits with minicameras hidden in their tie clasps; their secret societies and omnipresent spies; and those tiny soldiers in helmets and puttees shown in Fox newsreels cradling huge, heavy machine guns and mowing down the Chinese peasants. In the popular imagination, the model disciple of the Jesuits, the good student of 1880, and the "brave samurai" of 1905 gave way to an annoying little squirt whose appetite is starting to make people nervous.

But despite any truth this portrait might contain, it contained much more ignorance. Antipathy can never substitute for information, and you cannot grasp a people except through their character, even if it's in eclipse. No one knows much about the privations that Japan imposes on itself to build its arsenal for this war that seemed inevitable. On December 8, 1941 (it is the seventh in Washington) at eight o'clock in the morning, bombers and torpedo boats take off in waves from the aircraft carriers of Admiral Nagumo, destroying the American Pacific fleet at Pearl Harbor. An hour and a half later, the Japanese ambassador presents a declaration of war to the American government. Ninety minutes: that's about how long the attack lasted. For a good half of the Japanese pilots, this was a "holy war" they had begun, and many agree with Yosuke Matsuoka, minister of foreign affairs, that "the mission of the people of Yamato is to prevent the human race from becoming diabolic."

TOKYO, JUNE 1943

All able-bodied men are in the army, and many young women are working in the war plants of Nagoya or the coal mines of Kyūshū. Garbage is collected by old women, sometimes even by old priestesses torn from their monasteries. The women sweeping the main road in Ginza in June 1943 find two papers in the gutter.

The first is a page torn from a magazine, *Koron*. It says:

As long as Imperial Decree sustains the conviction that Japan is contemporary with Heaven and Earth, America will be condemned to destruction . . .

The second is a police order. It says:

Due to the power of modern explosives, we are sometimes required to abandon our efforts to find the remains of our dead. That is why we ask all families of soldiers who go into active duty to save a lock of hair or a fingernail clipping, in order to avoid the risk of not having kept anything of the body of an honored dead.

These objects—if they become relics—are taken to the Great Temple of Yasukuni, where all the soldiers who die for their country are revered as gods.

In territory that shrinks daily, Japanese officers sleep with their heads turned toward the Imperial Palace. After a series of hand-to-hand battles on the islands of the Pacific, the Americans are getting ready to land in Japan.

But will that happen? Surrender or a fight to the death? What role will the emperor play? How is the country coping with the bombings? What will the Japanese do?

YUJI SPEAKS, OR A LESSON IN "NOTHING"

———————●———————

Hiroshima, August 1945
Tokyo, October 1955

"HAVE I TOLD YOU"—his laugh sounds like a rattle—"that we had already lost our father? He was the professor of Japanese philosophy at the Imperial University, and he explained Confucian and Shintoist texts to his students, texts that had been officially predated by several centuries so they would owe nothing to China. Japan at the origin of the world . . . the Japanese engaged in a divine mission . . . you know all that. He knew the real explanation of this mumbo jumbo, and he was planning to correct this lie and publish his research, when Japan experienced the euphoria of its final victory—no one doubted it would occur when our navy was defeated, the press"—he laughs again—"had annihilated the enemy. Even after the first bombings, he didn't leave his worktable—my mother even brought him his meals there. One morning during the summer of 1944, leaving the shelter where she had taken my younger brother and me, we saw that the house had been hit, found my father sprawled near his office, his back broken, in a patch of sun. He looked like a dwarf. An injection brought him back to consciousness for a few minutes. He asked my mother—he loved her—to forgive him for dying in such a way, leaving her alone at this critical time. For us, the children, not a word, not a look. From this silence, I drew the conclusion that we were not the sons he would have chosen. The eldest, the only one of us who always obeyed, had disappeared at the Battle of Midway. Since my father never showed me any affection, this silence weighed heavily on me. After the funeral—Tokyo had become unbearable—we went down, the three of us, to my mother's family, sixty kilometers south of Hiroshima.

"I was excused from service—tuberculosis—and my brother, a student, was too young for a uniform, but the army had drafted him to work in a metal recycling plant. He was growing very fast and not eating enough. He got surly and belligerent. He was convinced that he suffered from a lack of sugar; in fact he suffered from a lack of everything—all he had in his mouth was complaint. He tried to pawn our belongings to buy some sugar—it was the cause of daily quarrels. Without my knowledge, he persuaded my mother to go and beg a few kilos from my uncle, who at that time was a doctor at the hospital in Hiroshima. The local peasants who had enough to eat paid in kind for their visits and medicine; so the doctors were paid mostly in provisions and traded any surplus. A journey of sixty kilometers was no small affair just then, and my mother was weak and sick, but my brother didn't have to beg too much—he was her favorite, as the youngest often is. So she set out, with a piece of ancient silk she planned to trade under her arm. Two days later, around noon, there was a strange glow in the sky to the north. We learned that a disaster had hit Hiroshima. There were all sorts of rumors about it. We arrived in the city on foot, my brother and I. Before we even reached the outskirts, the sky was gray with suspended soot. The earth was still warm. At the place where the hospital had been, there was a scribbled notice from the surviving doctors announcing a meeting in twenty days for the families of the sick and missing and recommending they get as far away as possible as quickly as possible. This was the first time I'd ever read the word for 'radiation' in Japanese. In the heart of the ruins, you could hear the humming of crickets and cicadas that, much more resistant than we, died singing.

"On the day of the meeting, we went back, the two of us and what was left of our family. There was a crowd around the notice: patched jackets, old army caps, feet bound with rags—a small primitive clan terrified by the totem that had fallen from the new sky. The ashes and the human bones collected in the hospital ruins were weighed on a scale and divided equally among the mourners so that the conventional funerary rites could take place. I don't remember seeing anyone crying, I think we were all too afraid: in this charred city there was a threat much greater than sobs and tears. After the distribution of the ashes and bones, everyone scattered in the evening snuffing out their grief. We started on the road home with our portion knotted in a hankerchief. On the way, my brother told me the story of the three kilos of sugar, told me of the remorse he felt, and that night he disappeared.

"The family council paid for the Buddhist ceremony and the tomb and then informed me that I shouldn't count on it for anything more. I began walking back to Tokyo, where I still had my father's house. I took the Nakasendō, the old route through central Japan, which had barely been touched by the war. In the Nagano mountains, it was already autumn: the fields were mauve with autumn crocus and scabious, the air spicy and delicious. The countryside is very beautiful there—we'll go there together someday if you have the time. The most isolated roads were full of wanderers like me, who kept alive on berries, fresh water, and myrtle, marching on ahead, a little randomly, on their straw sandals, to escape from a life reduced to ashes. That autumn, the Japanese had threadbare soles"— he laughs—"and walking does help to support the insupportable.

"I spent four months on the road and arrived in Tokyo just before Christmas. The city had been destroyed in the meantime and was no better off than Hiroshima. In the northern suburbs, the trees and houses scorched by the bombs shone under a fine coating of snow. Our house was still standing. When I got to the garden gate, I saw two silhouettes moving wildly on the porch. (I couldn't see well, I had broken my glasses on the way and had not been able to replace them.) One of them was holding an open knife—there was a kick and it went flying in a graceful flash of silver. The other person was my brother. He had teamed up with the Blackshirts who traded in the ruins, and together they had pillaged the house (where he had been staying). I was so tired from my trip that I fell asleep without asking for an explanation; I do not know how this quarrel ended. The next day the police arrested my brother and held him for a few weeks. The hoodlums from his gang gave me back half of the money they had earned with our belongings, and so I was able to take him a meal in prison each morning. Sorrow had unbalanced his mind, he could not forgive himself for the death of his mother, and as you know this type of emotion weighs heavily on us here. When he wasn't sleeping, he cried; it was impossible to talk reason with him. Me, his elder, I felt powerless to help him. Nothing is more frightening than a human being who is this lost. The day he was released, he left me a note saying that he had gone to rejoin our mother in the place where he had sent her, and I never heard a word from him again. He was eighteen years old.

"Peace returned, I found myself alone, with the ghost of my brother for a companion. Like my father, who had left me his silence, my brother had left me his sorrow: those three damned kilos of sugar weighed on my heart. I had to rid myself of them one way or another: to understand, accept, forgive. Who was responsible? Why did my brother kill himself? Who had produced this sinister scenario? Why my mother, who surely was the best of us all? I turned these questions over in my mind, as I traveled, still on foot, toward the island of Shikoku. Did the Christians have the answer? I took a job as interpreter for an American missionary who was building a school in the Kōchi province. I had little work and plenty to eat. I used my free time devouring the Bible, which I had just discovered. I even took it with me to the toilet. Lot, the fire in the sky over Sodom, Job...okay! But even Job didn't send his mother to the furnace to satisfy his taste for sugar, and he wasn't Japanese." (Laugh.) "The missionary, who knew my history and knew that I was in the toilet with his holy book, would pace in front of the closed door, in the stench of the latrines, no doubt waiting for me to discover the passage that would open my eyes. I would hear the creak of his shoes. I wish I'd found what I was searching for—for me, and also to give him a little of what I owed him. But I didn't find it. He meant well, but the extent of the disaster was bigger than both of us. And his doggedness in trying to convert me finally aggravated me and I left. I went to work in a Catholic hospital with no greater success, and I turned away from

Christianity. I set out again, walking toward the north, where I became the headmaster of a school in a village on the outskirts of Shizuoka. Four thousand yen a month, barely enough food, a communal dormitory where I had absolutely no desire to live. Solitude was a bad companion, but it was all I had left, and at least we knew each other. At this point in my life, company would have killed me more quickly.

"During the Meiji period, each province had been ordered to build a pavilion in a clearing for the contagiously ill people that the district hospital could not accept. Later, during Hirohito's reign, the epidemics subsided and these forest retreats were abandoned; although the State left a watchman at each one. I wanted to live in one of these deserted cabins and finally asked the elders where it was, since the land registry had burned. I found it after two hours of walking north of the city, where the hills covered in tea trees gave way to the forest. I found a young girl from Nagoya there too. After having lost her whole family, she'd had the same idea as I and had lived there for a few weeks. She washed the pots and pans at the city hospital, getting up at dawn to go to work. If we combined our two salaries and planted the old garden, we could get by. Like characters in a folktale, we were living on mushrooms and dead wood. The smell of the forest, the hooting of owls, and the cries of the foxes surrounded this rebirth. We were both as light as cinder and as hard as bamboo that has passed through a fire— nothing for regrets, hypocrisy, or melancholy to cling to. I don't know if I must speak of love." He laughs. "Every day we reinvented a little bit of life. When our little baby was two years old, we set out for Tokyo. It was in '48, I had started to work for the magazines that were starting up again. We moved ten times— you know the problem here. Our last home, behind the station of Yotsuya, not far from your room, belonged to a widow who had just converted to Christianity. She prayed all night to Saint Anthony of Padua, asking him to give back what life had taken from her: a husband, children, marriage kimonos, money. She shouted his name, crying, sobbing, stamping her foot, certainly never seeing anything she asked for. A person always expects more from a new religion." (Laugh.) "We couldn't tolerate it. When I complained, she threw us out. We put our few possessions in a handcart, and she hummed while she helped us fill it; she seemed to have forgotten Saint Anthony and her grief. Just as we were leaving, she said, 'Excuse me,' lifted my hand to her mouth as if to kiss it, and bit my palm, severing two tendons. To the priest and the police, she said that she couldn't stand to look at my face anymore." (Laughing, he shows me a thin white scar that angles across his lifeline.)

"We have been here at Meguro since the New Year. My wife has waited to fall sick again until I make enough to care for her. I make almost one hundred thousand yen a month with the magazines and my translation, I drink up a third of that—alcohol gives me a little space—and the part that's left is more than enough to live on. With Rimifon she will get well. We are like air for one another now, light, transparent, indispensable. If she dies first, as she sometimes threatens, I would not remarry, and I would have a terrible time keeping my spirits up. Do you recall the poem that the princess Oku wrote over a thousand years ago?

> 'How my Lord
> shall you clear
> the mountains of autumn all alone
> when it was so difficult
> to cross them together?'"

. . . We are kneeling face to face before a low table in their only room. I am editing an article that he placed for me yesterday afternoon and that we must deliver tomorrow. He translates the pages I hold out to him one by one onto a paper divided into four hundred rectangles—one per ideogram. It is the last page; the sun is rising, we have worked all night, voices lowered because his wife and his daughter are asleep on a mat next to us. After supper was served, they left for the public baths, returned with hair still wet. "*Oyasumi nasai,* sleep well." There they are, nice and warm under the eiderdown, rubbed down like young fillies; they twitch as they

dream, their feet touch ours. The little girl is a marvel at seven—
long chubby legs the color of gingerbread—she draws apples in
pastel like Cézanne. The mother has the smooth face of a phantom,
wonderful hair that falls to her hips, a contained gaity: her presence alone is a favor, she is the princess Oku. Yuji stretches, laughing while dawn paints with violet the cabbages that cast off in tight
rows just under the open window. Before leaving for work, our
neighbors, gray with sleep, scatter the contents of their lavatories
in their garden patch. Yuji, he is a small man, dry and musical, as
transparent as a snowflake. He has the look of an ether addict who
enjoys himself and dances, with the pale and troubling lightness
of someone who has passed through fire. I can easily see why someone bit his hand. When you meet a truly free person, you suddenly
feel so silly, with all your travels and projects . . .

   We went to deliver the article by the first train. Meguro, Akihabara, Yotsuya, Akabane . . . In Tokyo, life is expressed in terms
of train stations: small metro stations or stations on the "Chūō
Line," with high streetlamps under the new leaves. The last train
has passed—song of wooden sandals moving away and diminish-
ing, and the whistling song—three notes—of the hot soup merchant. Carts of the street peddlers are parked against the quay for
the night. Small people, small debts that a person forgets and then
finds again: Japanese Dickens with an ineffable sweetness. Above
the lights, some trees caught by the night while the branches stir
up memories, meetings, lies, and regrets. Stations arranged like a
constellation in a city that one engrains in his memory like a rosary
in the darkness . . .

WASHINGTON, 1944–1945

———————•———————

THE MORE QUESTIONS they asked, the more they realized that they understood nothing about the psychology of their adversary, that his future behavior was an enigma, that the "authorities" they consulted contradicted themselves . . . in short, the Americans of 1944 did not know who the Japanese were.

They asked one of the best anthropologists in the country, Ruth Benedict, to study the Japanese mentality, which posed so many problems for them, and they provided her with all the help she could have hoped for: archives, films, translators, Japanese-Americans who had been interned as suspects. She was an older woman, her hair white, who was professional to the core. Because of her training, she avoided the error the West so often falls into: wanting everything to fit into *our* categories. Plus she had the virtue of a good investigator, patience, and she knew how to suspend judgment until all the collected observations organized themselves according to their own logic, and the pieces of the puzzle spontaneously fell into place. She never set foot in the country, and that may have been an advantage for her: she had no preconceived ideas, none of those "antibodies" that a trip to Japan often produces, making understanding more difficult. In the preface to her study, *The Chrysanthemum and the Sword,* she pointed out that the Americans (even though they had long since fought the Sioux and Comanche) had never had as enigmatic an enemy; it was with this admission of ignorance that she started her work.

With remarkable objectivity, she made the same meticulous

study of this millennial culture as she would have for a newly discovered tribe of aborigines, or for a society that suddenly sprang fully formed from nowhere; or for an abstract mechanical problem. That was how she was able to pick apart the workings of the Japanese mind without missing any significant cogs, and to present the Japanese with the first portrait ever drawn by a foreign hand—with a rather dry and pensive pen—in which they were able to recognize themselves.

One exception: her Japan is a week without Sunday. Studying a people from a distance and after a war, she ignored almost all the good occasions—village festivals, banquets, revelries—where a whole array of happier Japanese qualities burst forth, to which this rigid society knows, when it can, how to give vent.

Her book influenced everything the next generation wrote about Japan and helped the American occupation avoid a number of errors.

For the Japanese, beaten, helpless, deprived of all the myths they had cherished during twenty years of ideological totalitarianism, this old woman, who seemed as remote as the moon, gave such a sympathetic description of their strengths and weaknesses, the coherence of their society and the submission it imposed on them, *and without seeming to have a grudge against them*—this old woman was a great comfort to them.

Toward the end of the occupation, there wasn't a Japanese city that didn't have its Ruth Benedict Club, not a university where her ideas weren't discussed. This fad is over, but it was thanks to her book that the paths, which had been divergent for so long, began to move toward each other slightly.

This has long-term importance: we can hardly progress further today in the art of destruction, but there are still roads to build in the art of understanding.

AT SEIBO HOSPITAL, TOKYO, DECEMBER 1964
TO MARCH 1965

Even when you look through a kinetoscope or magic lantern, you should not kid yourself: the most essential connections are formed beyond the rational mind and are only rarely expressed in books: they are found in the tattoos seen at the beach or the morgue; in the pressure of two hands on a shoulder at the railroad station, fingers that cling—maybe too long—to this warmth and elasticity; in the cards written by soldiers, addressed so indecipherably that they arrive by mistake at the homes of old fools who have never heard anything so tender; in the quietness of two faces sunk deep in a pillow, as if they would like to disappear there; in this rarely satisfied and deeply held desire of the dying to find the end of the maze and something to say; in a window about to open; in the face of a child dissolving in tears, lost in the murmur of a strange language.

Courage. We are much closer than we think, but we don't always remember it.

PART TWO

———————•———————

THE YEAR
OF THE MONKEY,
1956

"PASSEPARTOUT"

———●———

*We are painfully conscious of your sentiments today, you, Our subjects.
Therefore, We have decided, in accordance with the dictates of fate and of
the present time, to pave the road toward a great peace for generations to
come by enduring the unendurable and supporting the insupportable.*
(Imperial decree, broadcast August 15, 1945)

The party that gains the advantage is the Imperial Party.
(Japanese proverb)

I N T H E S E B R I E F sentences, the emperor had announced his own
surrender and put an end to the war. His message was received
with astonishment and respect in the heart of the country, where
the peasants surely still believed that this august voice was like
thunder or a hurricane. A good number of rustic souls interpreted
his message this way: the Japanese headquarters had not been up
to snuff—the emperor had gotten rid of the unfit and listened to a
better advisor, MacArthur. The order was understood: officers who
disapproved committed suicide; and the GIs disembarked, without firing a shot, upon a Japan in ashes; but at the entrance of a
destroyed village, they encountered children who had been posted
there to welcome them and wave flags . . . *Japanese flags.*

The occupation (1945–52) was a success. The Americans—
despite the extremist propaganda predicting terrible reprisals from
them—behaved with discipline and without rancor. They fed the
population; fueled the economy (a billion dollars in 1948);
imposed useful reforms; purged, then pardoned "those responsible"; and set it afloat again, this country that they had, in the
meantime, fallen in love with. Their natural good-heartedness,

their atomic "bad conscience," and their fear of Russian or Chinese communism all combined in the rapid transformation of ex-enemies into protégés. On their side, the Japanese made peace as they had formerly made war: expeditiously. They were the model occupied nation. Their energy and adaptability, together with a rejuvenated industry that was supplying the Americans for the Korean war, completed the recovery.

To sum it up, they had taken excellent advantage of the "American experience." But one grows weary of the same dish, however nourishing, on the table every day.

In 1955, their independence was restored, and satiated with America, the Japanese wanted to change the menu. They wanted some of the old culture, European, particularly French: this nation that had produced Renoir, Jean-Paul Sartre, Yves Montand, and romantic love, and that had, nonetheless, lost the war before they won it (endearing them still further). Each month, when the steamboat arrived from Marseilles, journalists invaded the lower deck and beseiged the commissioner for whatever he might have (no matter what: academics, ex-convicts, lettered poets) that they could sink their teeth into.

YOKOHAMA-TOKYO, OCTOBER 20, 1955

The arrival of the MM *Cambodia* this morning had not much to offer them: a ballad singer who "did" the style of Damia; a Mormon prophet who inundated the boat with mauve brochures promising the end of the world (1986 exactly) and invited everyone to prayer and contrition; a fellow who got on board in Sri Lanka, who did servile work in the ship's bowels to pay the price of his passage and who apparently had spent a long time on the tracks of Asia. But to what goal? The commissioner didn't know.

I didn't even hear the ship berth and the gangway descend. For three days, in a torrid hold under the kitchen, I had used a knife and a steam jet to remove fat from serving platters and dripping-pans the size of coffins, assisted by Alcide and Francis, two black men from Martinique who kept up a dialogue all day in a flowery, nicely antiquated French that was riddled with nursery rhymes, proverbs, rustic images, and devoted exclusively to the penis's penetration of the vagina. These charming, erotic litanies made the time pass quickly. To think incessantly of lovemaking, like this, in the middle of this grease, seemed truly the sign of natural happiness. All the more since the stink and the heat made the work so hard that it was often necessary to pause and vomit the "Turbot supreme" or the "Marengo soufflé" that we had taken from the ovens of the huge kitchen. In the yellow haze and grease of our cabin, I just barely recognized the stripes of the commissioner who came to find me.

Good-bye, Francis. Good-bye, Alcide. Have fun, children. I will let you guess the wishes these two troubadors offered (without parting from their favorite theme) for my sojourn here.

Captain Cook had a sword and saluted the Maori chiefs with a cocked hat as brilliant as the sun. La Pérouse randomly distributed iron axes and blue glass pearls. Phileas Fogg kept a pigskin suitcase stuffed with bank notes by his side. I arrived on the sooty bridge like a tallow candle with nothing to offer but the dishcloth I had in my hand. Traveling had changed.

The weather was superb—bright white seagulls in the sun of October, the best month in Japan. Cameras flashed. A half-dozen small men with pronounced faces were already surrounding me, asking questions, without embarrassment, in "japanglish": Who was I? Why come here? What did I want to do? What did I expect from this country?

At the time, it was revolutionary—travelers of my kind all stayed in the ashrams of India, they hadn't arrived here yet. My interlocutors were almost as threadbare as I—worn jackets, eyeglass frames repaired with tape. But their "made in Japan" cameras were already instruments of precision, and their expressions lively, precise, and frankly amiable. One of them (whom I was later to get to know) was named Yuji. "This will be hard, very hard, it will not be easy going all alone," he said to me with small bows that appeared neither comic nor obsequious, "and do you really have any idea what kind of lives we lead here?"

Hard? Here, at least it's cool! I had just spent eight months in the tropics, confined by heat and malaria in a worm-eaten inn that the termites were quickly transforming into sawdust. The air of Yokohama felt like champagne.

Fortunately, I didn't have too many expectations.

As for my knowledge, it was too limited to bother me much. In Delhi, Colombo, Saigon, I had met the obliging and taciturn consuls, who tapped their sweaty faces with little dry strokes of immaculate handkerchiefs; washed their hands a hundred times a day; and made you think of surgeons, lost without disinfectant or instructions in the limp and long-winded agitation of Southeast Asia.

As a child, I had seen "Japanese shells" open at the bottom of a glass of water and send their red-and-white flowers toward the surface, crammed with tiny buoys of elder; and although I never received models, I had dog-eared the Christmas toy catalogues that showed them, the two biggest battleships in the world on a 1/1000 scale—the *Musashi* and the *Yamato*—which are now at the bottom of the sea. Later, I heard Madame Butterfly sing (in Italian) her desperation at having been left; and, like the Impressionists, I looked at a few prints, certainly not the best. I also remembered an episode from *Around the World in Eighty Days,* where Passepartout spotted his master among the ranks of spectators and left his place in the "human pyramid" of the Yokohama circus, without permission, which led to the collapse of the entire structure and caused him to lose face with his employers. But I hadn't realized how much of the true Japanese was contained in the moral of the story.

Here's to innocents with their hands full.

I disembarked, checked my baggage at Tokyo-Central, and set out to wander this interminable city with a toothbrush in my pocket. It was a joy to walk down these long avenues, refreshed by the wind, looking at the faces. All the women had a freshly washed look, all the passersby seem on their way toward a precise destination, all the workers work, and there are minuscule shops everywhere offering, for a few yen, a good, strong cup of coffee: after two years in Asia, I had stopped believing in such small miracles.

I have twelve dollars in my pocket. Out of curiosity, I make the rounds of the "Western-style" hotels to find out how many nights' lodging I can afford in this capital: one and a half at Dai-ichi, full of redheaded GIs with wrists like logs; one and a quarter at the Prince Hotel; barely one at the Imperial, built by Frank Lloyd Wright in Inca or "Atlantis" style, on sliding foundations that survived the earthquake of 1923. And almost a week at the Japanese inns north of the station, which offer mats and parchment finishes, at six hundred yen per day. It is still too much.

That afternoon, I walk through the city, twelve miles at random. The air is delicious. I see, in passing, an exhibit of Japanese photos, with a style so detailed that everything is forever frozen in them. I watch fire trucks pass at full speed through clouds of dead leaves, their bronze bells pealing as if they are on their way to a party, with a cluster of small men in black and red holding on to ladders, wearing hats with neck protectors like the warriors of Genghis Khan. I rest at the foot of a Russian church, listening to the choir, big and passionate enough to absorb the whole city. These aimless avenues, the depots, the bookstores crammed with standing readers, this maze of small gardens, of tiny, unequal houses that butt up against a stagnant canal, against a backdrop of ultramodern buildings, against the railroad ballast . . . after eight hours of walking, I ask myself if these things make a beautiful city, or a city at all. Then the sun sets against an orange sky—throwing into silhouette the incongruous lines of the rooftops, the crazy scribbling of antennas, of electric wires and ad balloons, against a horizon that becomes red, then the multicolored rain of neon. I stop asking myself questions.

From the Russian church, it's downhill. The slope and the fatigue help me, and around eleven o'clock in the evening I find myself in the small quarter of Surugadai, in a perfume of roasted coffee and grilled brochettes. The narrow streets are packed—families carrying their sleeping children, streetlights, neon signs, carts hung with acetylene lamps where loud shouts sell remaindered cotton fabric at cheap prices, rubber boots, plastic or bamboo toys. On both sides of the street, cases of jumbled rubbish spill their contents onto the sidewalk. Bistros, one next to the other. But all that is unimportant: I am hungry. I push open a door marked Café-Bar Shi. *Shi,* I asked, means poem. That didn't shock me at all: in my walk I had already chanced upon two Rilke tearooms, a François Villon snack bar, a Rimbaud pool hall, and a Julien Sorel store (saucy lingerie). They have advanced tastes here. In an area not much larger than an armchair, it hardly surprised me to see three Daumier engravings and to hear a record player murmuring Ravel. A Lilliputian barmaid, well cared for and plump, made up from head to toe, as personal as a paper rose. A clientele of high schoolers, bare feet in wooden sandals, in black uniforms, with black caps; they are spelling, plunged into their black schoolbooks, fighting against sleepiness. I had just enough time to think: seminarians...Chekhov—and I fell asleep on a tiny chair without even placing my order.

The owner woke me at about one in the morning. The room was empty and the light extinguished. With one hand he balanced a bicycle that must have been hidden behind the bar; in the other was a glass of milk that he put down in front of me. A young and timid air. "My name is Shoji," he said in poor English, "unemployed engineer and bartender while looking for work. If you'd like to sleep on a table, feel free. I'm going home, I've got two hours of riding to do. The toilets are next to the bar. I'll see you tomorrow." He left and closed the door behind him.

From time to time, a late-nighter entered the public baths next door, and I heard the song of wooden sandals—click, clack, click, clack—advancing and receding in the alley.

Waiting to fall back to sleep, I skimmed through the evening newspaper I had bought during my walk. A few articles started with: We Japanese, we do not know how to do this...We would do well to try to...It is necessary to correct this national fault, etc. But I could feel that their heart was no longer in it and that the time for peccavi had passed. More common were the stories of escaped prisoners returning from Russia and of all those people still living on windfalls and wiles—ingenious swindlers with assumed identities or in jobs that weren't theirs. But these aliases, these improvisations, these picaresque existences stimulated ideas and created an open and lively climate. I had the impression that more than a few ancient impostures had flown away with the defeat and had not settled again. The advertisements of Japanese schoolchildren in search of stamp exchanges or pen pals filled an entire page. The rice harvest of 1955 had beaten all records. Life was still difficult, but the "economic miracle" was starting to pay its dividends, and Japan was starting to believe in its luck again.

I go to examine the packs of cigarettes carefully lined up under the bar; they are called "Peace," "Love," "Sincerity," "Pearl," "New Life." Perhaps it is the right time to land here.

AROUND ARAKI-CHO

———————•———————

NOT EASY TO FIND a room here. A foreigner is obviously
rich, he can travel. The serious agents offered me fifteen-
room villas; the less serious ones also refused to believe that a
foreigner could be interested in a room measuring four mats (4.6
square yards), and usually ended up offering me women. When
they happened to have something, it was necessary to pay them up
front, the *shkikin* (guarantee), the *ken rikin* (key deposit), and the
tesuryo (commission), which equaled ten months' rent.

Better to search door to door and neighborhood by neighborhood through the biggest capital of the world, sleeping each night
in a quarter with a different name—Akihabara (the plain of autumn
leaves), Yotsuya (four valleys), Ochanomizu (tea water), Nabeya
yokocho (the crossroad of the pothole)—every day more exhausted
but more enamored of this sea of pug faces, oiled lanterns, laun-
dries, tiny houses of gray wood leaning one against the other in the
bitter, iodized smoke of Japanese cooking. I tried this for seven
days, without success. On the eighth, the owner of the "Poem Bar"
found something for me. I bought a straw mattress, a quilt, a
small pillow filled with rice balls (all you need to move in here) and
settled myself into the home of a night watchman in the Araki-cho
quarter for a year.

Cho is a small quarter; *ki,* wood or tree; and *ara* is a type of berry.
But there aren't any more berry trees in Araki-cho.

Sunflowers, bamboo, wisteria. Tilting, worm-eaten houses.
Smell of sawdust, green tea, salt cod. At dawn, from all sides, the

ruffled song of roosters. Omnipresent advertising hideously incorporating the most beautiful writing in the world.

Araki-cho is, in sum, a forgotten bit of village within the city; in the past, four first-class geisha houses had made it famous. They had been burned down, like most of the others, leaving only a small "school" to which a handful of suffering, fussy young women come, knees bent from their high wooden shoes, to learn to play *shamisen*, to walk so each step is made up of twenty-six distinct movements, and to be at ease with both classic poetry and libertine innuendo. But today, the city's directory of geishas shows it to be at the bottom level—the very borders of gallantry—and the quarter has long since cast aside those memories. It is not marked on any map, and the taxi drivers who skirt its borders rarely even know its name.

Two very distinct mentalities can be seen in Tokyo. The southern and eastern parts of the city—home of barge owners, fishmongers, and grocers, and artisans whose tools have not changed for a hundred years—have the *shitamachi* (low city) spirit. Cheeky and heartfelt. It is the *shitamachi* who applaud the *sumo* wrestlers with their chignons, who feed the gossip columns and sniff and sob over the drama of the Kabuki theater. Who carry the flavor of the old folklore of Edo. The more well-to-do areas of the west and north have the *yamanote* (next-to-the-hills) spirit—more bourgeois, studious, preserved. *Yamanote* are interested in the traditional arts: calligraphy, Noh theater. They embrace the West, sitting under a hanging brass lamp to read European books. Much in the spirit of the Meiji era.

Araki-cho is *yamanote* by geography and *shitamachi* in spirit, with an extra touch of rusticity. There are no foreigners there, and the only English words that have entered the local language are *kissu* (from "kiss"), which goes back to prewar times, and *stenko* (from "stinky"), which is a word that is especially apt whenever rain floods the septic tanks (no sewage systems before 1970) or when the cesspool cleaners go on strike. Araki-cho is still in the bull's-eye of the huge target of "Greater Tokyo," only six train stations from the Imperial Palace. You get off at the Ichigaya station,

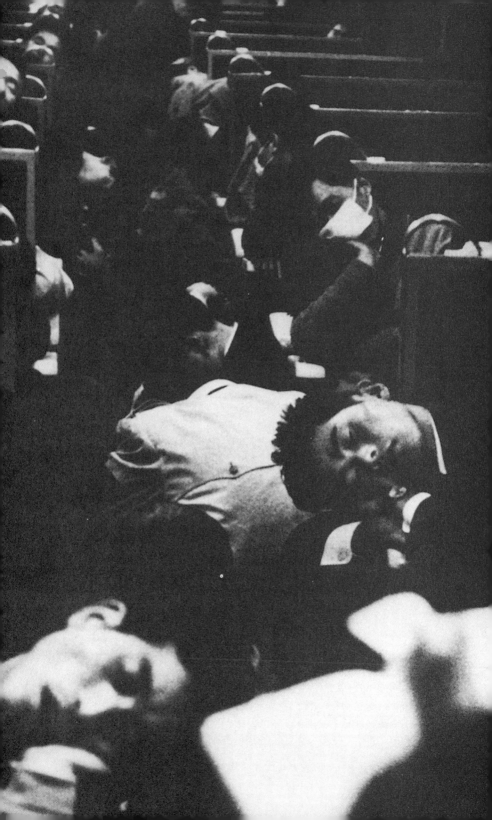

and for ten minutes follow a canal sheltered by mastic trees, where lovers paddle timidly in rented canoes on full moon evenings. At the intersection of two avenues, you reach a sake bar where a narrow alley carries you up to the plateau of Araki-cho.

At the foot of the only commercial street is the Café-Life: somber, cramped, perfect for starting the day. The old woman with the carefully coiled hair who runs the store never opens her mouth except to excuse herself, pronouncing all the final syllables that the young, busy urbanites are starting to drop. But under her submissive look, she is hard as a brick, and everyone here knows how she lords it over her husband, an ex-sergeant. When he strikes back, she suffers a good shiner with dignity. *Sengo tsuyoku natta no wa: onna to stocking* (since the war, two things are more resistant: women and stockings). This is sometimes said with resignation; but the strength of the women, in any case, is nothing new.

The Café Life, whose clients belong to the street, have a French record:

> *Dis-moi donc, Jenny La Chance*
> *Pourquoi les m'sieurs qu'tu connais bien*
> *Quand ils te croisent le dimanche*
> *Te r'gardent comme des . . . r'gardent comme des . . .*
> *R'gardent comme des (the needle skips)*
> *Sa-cris-tains . . .*

I ask myself how "Jenny La Chance" ended up here. It was an old recording, its exoticism already worn out, and no one understood the words; not important, it is *furanzu* (French), so they like it.

Down the street, a Shinto sanctuary dedicated to Inari, the Goddess of Food, and to her helper and messenger, Kitsune the fox, shares the bottom of a small grassy ravine with a sawmill. When it's quiet, through a thin cloud of incense, you can hear the yapping of *Kamishibai san* (Mr. Theater-in-Paper) entrancing his audience of children. He inserts a dozen cardboard images into the box attached to his bicycle, then pulls them out one at a time to illustrate the story that he chants in an unbelievably rough voice—

now plaintive, now menacing. Ogres, gangsters, dragons, duels. Styles and mythologies are liberally mixed: one sees a tiger romping at the feet of the Virgin Mary, a samurai piloting a submarine. When a big enough audience is gathered, the one-man theater interrupts his story and sells waffles at five yen apiece. On good days, with a fresh tale, he makes a quick two hundred and just as quickly goes to get drunk: the job makes him thirsty, and the competition of television worries him.

The houses of Araki-cho don't have locks, or the locks are so flimsy a child could jimmy them. The cardboard doors gape open onto narrow antechambers where the occupants line up their shoes, pointed toward the outside. It's practical: just a quick look in passing to see if Tanaka or Morita is at home. Sometimes a thief (not from the quarter) passes through during siesta hour and disappears like a zephyr with the best pairs. Quite a blow, since the convenient shoes still cost a quarter of a worker's salary; but no one wants to bother the police for so little.

The police station is located just inside the quarter at K Avenue. Each resident has a dossier there—birthplace, age, police record, reputation, conduct, etc.—which the go-betweens for arranged marriages use to carefully verify the honor of their clients. Outside of an hour of judo each day, the three cops have nothing to do except draw detailed maps in their notebooks for the poor guy trying to find an address—since most of the streets in Tokyo lack names, and the houses are not numbered in sequence, only with the construction date. To kill time on long afternoons, they sink into interminable games of go (it is a sort of Halma but much more subtle, where a player's tokens are placed according to extremely treacherous maneuvers, aimed at encircling and eliminating those of his opponent). When a player finds himself in one of these critical situations where the greatest caution is required, he telephones the cops at the next station, who jump in their police cars and speed, full steam, to examine the board and lend him a hand. When you hear their siren, it's usually for this purpose: Araki-cho is a quiet quarter.

If the police want a fight, they can always go to the local

cinema: it is next door. Fifty yen a seat, first showing at nine in the morning. The audience sits cross-legged on hard wood seats. Despite the law against it, the air is thick with smoke; but everyone hides his cigarettes, and this carefulness shows sufficient respect for the law. They will certainly show the *chambara* (samurai films), generally slapped together in three weeks, which are to Japan what Westerns are to the United States. Sometimes during the summer, they show ghost movies: sinister legends of feudal Japan, full of magic and apparitions that float through the nocturnal air searching for human prey, their foreheads marked with a triangular braid under a gigantic shock of red hair that has a truly terrifying effect.

Though the common mood is optimistic, reality here carries its own ghosts—just as terrifying. The radioactivity level in the rain is front page news, especially when it reaches one hundred times normal from a western wind—a bomb in Siberia (today in Red China). Faces and nerves tighten. There are typhoons in August and September, with charming female names: Sybill, Sylvia, whose capricious itineraries are broadcast on the half hour while people survey the black sky and tie down their flimsy roofs, well designed for flying away, with straw ropes. There are mornings when the ground trembles, when a malevolent hand shakes the houses as if knocking fruit from a tree. When the second shock wave heaves up through the floorboards, I see my neighbors rush down their wooden stairs with unrecognizable faces: pallid, closed like fists, and more frightening than the earthquake itself. "Magnitude 3," says the headline in the evening newspapers. Three out of a possible eight, which none of the jolts has ever reached. The scale is logarithmic, so three is one hundred times as strong as one. In 1923, a quake between four and five totally destroyed Tokyo. This time there were no victims other than the red fish thrown out of their pool, agonizing in silence on the green grass.

Then, there is the price of rice, which affects the small budgets and the mood of the quarter. No one begs in Araki-cho; they are discreet about the sacrifices that they impose on themselves to preserve an honorable face and keep their children properly dressed. The ice is thin, there is nothing in reserve, and the balance is so precarious that the smallest mishap—a missed exam, an illness, a parent who fails in his duty—can push a person over the edge and send the marriage kimono or the television "straight as an arrow" to *ichi-roku-ginko* (literally: the bank of the six percent a month), the "cooler."

Do not take risks, speak only to your own class, don't do anything inconsiderate: everything marches to a careful prudence taught by the bad luck that so often afflicts the little people of the big cities—and the universes of Dickens or Zola.

For the people of Araki-cho, the big city is none other than Tokyo, where they rarely go; instead they go to Shinjuku, where the lights redden the sky, fifteen minutes west on foot. Satellite city, shopping center, and train crossroads for the suburbs, Shinjuku is also one of those pleasure quarters found in the Far East. Tokyo has four: Ginza, the most sophisticated, chosen by the foreigner in need of nightlife; Asakusa, simultaneously bigoted and libertine, where a visit to the Buddhist temple of the goddess Kwannon serves as the auspicious prelude to more earthly diversions; Ikebukuro, sordid and violent; and Shinjuku, whose seductions were judged so harmful by the regents of Tokugawa that they have razed it and planted it with rice fields—twice. Each time it has come back, it has become more marginal: popular theaters, movie clubs, grills, Chinese lotteries, mah-jongg rooms, foreign bookstores open until ten o'clock where one can stand and read without ever buying anything, wood-and-straw taverns where shellfish is cooked in the best sake in Japan, a whole population of soothsayers, fortune tellers, palm readers, set up in the streets under the light of a lantern, who confidently proffer much-needed reasons to hope. Add to this the three floors of the Donskoi bistro (title of a novel by Gorky), where the sentimental left, served by students in Russian blouses, come to recite Mayakovski, listen to Brecht, sing *yanagibushi,* those couplets of pain and difficulty that the old Japanese workers sang . . . and to step out a little before fading back into the crowd. Rats, garbage, and striptease. Finally, the café-disco Fugetsudo (the moon in the window), filled with bohemians in Basque berets, of ambiguous gender, where one can listen to any

classical work from Palestrina to Schönberg. At the end of the quarter, three parallel streets lined with giant lanterns, a strong smell
of herbal medicine, disinfectant, cheap perfume. Since 1958, the
after-dark houses have been closed, alas! But in the Year of the
Monkey this is where they were found. One heard breathing and
murmuring from the street and, through one side of a double door,
half open, the passerby could see Monet's *Olympia*, a mosaic decorating the back wall, and some enormous cast-iron tea urns
hissing on the braziers. Every Sunday, a car with a loudspeaker,
belonging to a feminist group, travels slowly through the alleys
while a polite voice repeats into the microphone: "It is a sin to sell
your body." The girls look and laugh: "It is an even bigger sin to
deny your parents their due." Many of them perform this work so
they can help their families or pay for the university tuition for a
brother, strutting around with a student's cap in similar streets at
the other end of the city. Standing on the stoop, in tight skirts,
they take in the air, gulping milk from the bottle, or busy themselves with a baby, giving their neighbor time to do her shopping.
Most often, they are peasants driven by poverty from the provinces
of the Northeast. They do their best to relieve boredom of a city
dweller's life, hope to free themselves in a season or two and open a
small business in the city, or return to the country of Iwate or
Aomori ken with a few teeth filled with gold, some baubles from
the capital, and enough money to find a husband. Often they manage to do just that, and no one up there cares anything for their
past. And as the Geisha says in *The Honorable Country Outing*:

*What difference is there between a married woman and an o-joro san
(prostitute)? Neither can choose her destiny: it is the gentleman, their
father who makes all the profit . . .* (Thomas Raucaut)

Not many delinquents in Shinjuku. All the same, the police
sometimes block a road or a cinema to check identification papers
and direct everyone to the station, where they pass several hours
smoking and joking with the old crippled Crainquebilles, street

peddlers truly vexed that they've been caught, who protest by waving their permits: expired, falsified, curled from perspiration. The sun shines golden on the floor of the police station. Sometimes a cop gets up to put the teapot on or they reprimand someone—they love it—but it is not often that they draw up a report. The easygoing mood is a cross between Brueghel and Hokusai.

As everyone knows, police raids draw people together, and in the floating world of Shinjuku, even a foreigner can make friends. It is more delicate in Araki-cho. Not that they would be xenophobic there, but they attribute a number of exotic habits to a foreigner, incongruous appetites and whims, sources of problems and puzzles. Several months passed while they observe me without lowering their guard. Relations here are rarely born of individual whim; they are almost always the result of sponsorship, of adoption, of group consensus in one form or another. I had learned what I could of spoken Japanese; as for the written, the newspapers employ no more than two thousand ideograms that make up a kind of demotic requiring many years of study. I had started by memorizing the proverbs. All the Japanese proverbs about unhappiness, disappointment, or bad luck are powerful expressions. "A bee sting on a face in tears" works better than our "Misfortunes never come singly." As for all the rest, they are as sententious, flat, and stale as our proverbs; but they have the advantage of being known and used by the Japanese masses for at least three generations. A proverb does not necessarily have to signify anything, its function is to reassure: at least you know where you're headed! In any case, they work wonders. Each time I use them judiciously, I am greeted by the same incredulous stupor that always greets the foreigner with the slightest amount of tact, knowledge, or timing: *O-djosu neee!* (Isn't he talented!). This exact phrase can also signify: "Work hard, you still need a lot." But it is not in this sense that it was used here, they were not at all malicious—only wary, and not very disposed to entering into a relationship without having already figured out a way to get out.

Another way to their hearts is to be very attentive to your body.

My landlords sleep on mattresses, four in one bedroom, with their feet literally on the neck of their neighbor. In the house next door it is the same. But this promiscuity has no odor, because in Japan cleanliness doesn't cost anything: one can bleach and starch a shirt for the price of a beautiful apple and spend two evenings at the *sento* (public baths) for the price of a cup of coffee. If forced, a Japanese can commit a few swindles, suffer the vicissitudes, and still count on indulgence, but if he doesn't go to the baths every night, he is doomed. This is even more true of foreigners who, since the first Portuguese and Dutch, have had the reputation of being so conspicuously dirty that they can be easily tracked by their odor. The pleasure that the Japanese take in ablutions of any kind has as much to do with rite as with hygiene. When the quarter holds *matsuri*—a propitiatory festival, the most awaited of the year; the usually sober men get drunk and march, staggering through the narrow streets carrying a heavy shrine that sweeps away sickness and demons—this rite is also a matter of cleansing.

Same joviality at *sento,* where the quarter gathers every evening.

In the side for men, the room is jammed with mirrors where the local youth study and compare their biceps. It costs twenty-three yen to enter, you receive a basket to store your clothes, and then, crouched in front of the faucets on ramps that surround the pool, you soap up and rinse before going to the boiling pool (118 to 125 degrees Fahrenheit) and joining your suddenly expansive and talkative neighbors. Nowhere else will you find the Japanese more accessible. Certain deputies profit from this "relaxation," taking up to ten baths a day before an election to brainwash blissful and receptive voters in water up to their chins.

At Araki-cho *sento,* the most popular hour is when the local cinema lets out. The young arrive in bands: tough guys, nostalgic or dazzled by the film that they have just seen, occupy the pool and make waves. Around midnight, there are places left for the peaceful, for the true connoisseurs who steep, eyes closed, or amuse themselves with games—plastic swans, miniature submarines— left behind by the kids. The elite of the quarter: the postman and the policeman, who finish their day late; the fishmonger, who goes

down to the big Tsukiji market auction every morning at four
o'clock to get his fish, and gets his sleep in the afternoon; and
Kamishibai, the puppeteer, who prefers discreet bathing because he
spent the war on an atoll where no one could see anything coming,
and out of carelessness and boredom, along with the rest of his pla-
toon, he had had his whole body tattooed with military slogans
that are now outdated and laughed at.

The women's side is not separated except by a half-partition
with open fretwork through which one can exchange familiar
jibes, soap, and massage gloves. In the past, everyone bathed
together; this partition was a concession made to the puritan West
at a time when Japan wanted to please them so badly. It is superflu-
ous. The Japanese are not troubled by nudity at the baths; they are
too accustomed to it, and if, on occasion, it is arousing, so what!
where's the harm? On this subject, they are more natural than we.
They have long been perplexed by our society, which puts on long
underwear and makes all sorts of fuss about getting in the
water... and then garnishes public gardens with opulent nude
women representing Commerce and Industry.

Like all Japanese, the people of Araki-cho are avid photographers, not artistic, but keen. Anyone born to these ideograms
would find something in this fad. Since the photos of my neighbors are all similar, it appears that photography is used to preserve
a souvenir of memorable times—marriages, visits to the "preserved
landscapes," awarding of diplomas—when one is much too absorbed
by the organization or by the etiquette to savor the pleasure. There
is a penchant toward life lived in the retrospective, which is easier
than the present, and a passion for photo albums. When visiting,
I am barely settled before I have one on my knees—the does of
Nara, the Aso volcano, the temples of Nikko—intended to smooth
out the first minutes of embarrassment and to furnish me with a
topic of conversation free of thorns.

These albums (I have seen a good hundred at least) have taught
me more about this country than the works of the greatest photographers. I often have a hard time identifying my host, since the
focus is on the eldest son, or a superior placed a good yard in front

of the group, which is blurred . . . my host is likely in a deferential haze, oh well. I look at the uncle, or at the elders with disciplined chignons standing directly in front of the temple facade, or at the fat-cheeked marmots wearing gloomy black high-school caps. Turning the pages, I see life stretching the skin of these faces, which get thin and taut, charged with a look that suggests a Japan that is frugal, introverted, and pathetic, certainly not the Japan of the brochures.

On my street, every family, even the poorest, has his camera displayed conspicuously, just as we show off our marriage veils. Today they would all have Minoltas. At this time, it is often the modest "box" series, cameras so deceiving that even subjects photographed up close come out tiny on the negative. I am the only one to possess a decent camera, and I am often asked for a favor: the tobacco merchant wants a "posed" photo; here and there someone wants a souvenir of the baby before the first haircut, since the warm season is approaching, and rashes too; the hairdresser dreams of sending an attractive portrait to her lover, who almost never writes anymore. I can still see her face: a small, fragile, pale woman who doesn't overestimate her chance to please, and whom, after the curling iron, against a darkened background, and in the glow of the flash, I transformed into a kind of sickly Yvonne Printemps.

In Araki-cho, no one accepts a favor without returning it, and my efforts earned some small presents: two eggs, a box of crabs, an Australian stamp, a pear that I found in front of my door when I returned home one night, wrapped up like a diamond. I collect these treasures, ready to do anything photographic before the doors that are starting to open halfway.

April: the spring is early and hurried. The abrupt heaviness of May. The monsoons of June: the *nyubai*. Every evening the sky turns dark, and the rain moves in. It can be heard everywhere resonating off the oiled paper of the umbrellas. The air is saturated with humidity; nothing will dry. July comes, and the temperature rises to 85 or 95 degrees in the houses. In the back of their workshops, the elders lie down on their sides, stomachs bare, and sigh: *Saa . . . atsui!* (It is so hot!). To give themselves courage, they attach small bronze bells over the threshold—the beautiful sound "refreshes" them. Difficult period: the heat saps energy, the *nyubai* attacks the nerves, and beneath an apparent solemnity, people are irascible and vindictive. The other evening, the three policemen of our station—those peaceable go players—had so harshly trashed a prostitute who insulted them that she died. After some embarrassing explanations, they were transferred. I found this out only by accident in the newspaper, since I am definitely the last one to be told such a story here. Stroke and eczema seem to be the way of the world: on the roads drivers with heavy loads fall asleep at the wheel and transform their tank trucks into coffins. Suicide tolls go up and crooked lending also. Commerce languishes. In the homes of the most destitute, the *obasan* (the grandmother, who is less easily taken in) is already headed in the direction of the pawnbroker, her feet dragging, a bundle of belongings under her arm. Bad times.

Ota san, my landlord, visited me the other day to "inquire about my health." A delicate but pointed way of reminding me that I owed him a payment. His business leaves something to be desired; the hideous little office desks he makes are not selling at all at the moment: who would want to squeeze their legs under a table and work in this furnace? Not me. There are already wagers that the Japanese magazines won't buy a line from me. While waiting for my luck to change, I live on sixty yen (one French franc) per day: ten to the cleaners (important), twenty-three for the public bath (indispensable), ten for bread, ten for milk, and an egg (weighed) at seven yen, when I find one that is small enough. I roll my cigarettes in airmail paper with a pinch of old pipe tobacco and glue them with boiled rice. When Ota san sees them—no one rolls cigarettes here—he lets out an irrepressible, childish, delicious laugh. With his old wrinkled face, his darned socks, his suit that "pouches"—at the seams, in the knees, the rear—and with his yellow, gaping teeth, he has the look of a good, salacious rabbit— a little moth-eaten. I offer him a cigarette, which he puts in his wallet like a relic, and which he has—no doubt—shown all around. Not one word on the subject of rent. From that day on the quarter changed, it opened up, letting me see its weakness, which it had kept modestly hidden. Someone recounted the story of the three policemen, which I already knew: a man who rolls his cigarettes can certainly understand a moment of anger. He won't risk humiliating anyone. They moved together to make room for me. Easy enough for one so thin. For the fat, it would take too much pushing.

THE FOOT
OF THE WALL

●

The Rat, the Hare, the Horse, the Rooster,
the Cow, the Dragon, the Sheep, the Dog,
the Tiger, the Snake, the Monkey, the Boar

THE JAPANESE use this ancient Chinese zodiac cycle to deter-
mine years, months, and hours of the day. 1956 was the Year
of the Monkey; 1966 was the Year of the Horse of Fire, when bearing daughters was not at all advisable.

The Month of the Sheep, in the Year of the Monkey, I thought I
was all set when a magazine asked me for twenty pages (which
would be twenty thousand yen payable on delivery) on . . . Erasmus
and Calvin! Japan is a country of booms, and this summer it was
in the grip of a "culture boom." Every day, new reviews started up
to inform Japan about the most rare, subtle, and sophisticated
foreign products. Every day, reviews disappeared again, without
publishing a third edition. They had budgets that were too tight,
microscopic offices, editors who were starving and charming—and
had unbounded ambitions. Dante, Balzac, Shakespeare? Too well
known, all that! only good for those who read in the metro. No:
they wanted the abstruse, the tenuous, the farfetched: Sénancour
rather than Rousseau, Buxtehude rather than Bach. So, Erasmus
and Calvin. Fortunately, there are libraries in Tokyo, where I spent
my last few coins to turn up opinions on these two characters more
authoritative than my own. When I went to deliver my article—on
foot, an hour's walk—in an alley of the Kanda quarter, I found
the editorial staff bankrupt, the office closed, and the director
absent. By the end of the afternoon, I had tracked him down: he
had already been hired as a general writer for an *ero-zashi* (erotic

magazine). He quickly grabbed his jacket and steered me to a café.
I put my manuscript under his nose: "What am I going to do with
Calvin? I can't eat it! And I don't have any more yen." He stroked
his chin for a minute, his eyes closed, murmuring *"Komatta koto
naa"* (this is something that makes me blush), then suggested that
I extract two or three pages—"changing the genre, you know: the
baths, the women . . . like Brantome, no?"—and he would make a
proposal to his new boss. But I didn't have the energy to pull anyone, even Erasmus, toward lechery. Clearly, it was too hot. My
spirit emptied by the summer, I stared long and hard at my ham-
burger; it would be my last for a long time.

"Why don't you let your troops sleep a little after spending three
days without rest?" an American journalist asked a Japanese officer
during the Chinese campaign.

He listened and responded: "But my soldiers know quite well
how to sleep, it is the opposite they must learn."

I had begun to understand how to eat Japanese-style; all that
was left was to learn how to not eat at all. In the two months that
followed the war, the Japanese had piled into the trains for the
country in order to go and exchange their last family relics for two
turnips or three eggs, and all my neighbors of Araki-cho had gone
through this. Moreover, a total deprivation is the best way for the
traveler to conquer his last hesitation toward a foreign cuisine.
By the end of one week of "dieting," the fumes and flavors that had
seemed suspect not so long before went straight to the stomach.
Soon there will be no question, I will eat *everything: daikon* and
renkon—huge, obscene, yellow turnips with a strong, sour taste
that can only be eaten mashed up in brine; algae broth; raw mollusk
(*tabiebi*) cut in rounds; huge blackened clams (*sasae*), so bitter even
the sake doesn't sweeten them. It's the same with the *misoshiro,* the
red bean soup served for breakfast, which gives off bitter and burnt
fumes that had often made my stomach turn—I now liked it at a
distance. I have become acclimated.

When things turn bad, rather than expecting too much from
people, one must sharpen one's relations with things. It was a simple wall that helped me out. The length of tram line seven, in the

Azabu quarter: the interminable journey that I had made on foot for several days to get my mail. I sat on a garbage can to rest, and raising my eyes, I saw: a long, stone wall festooned like a theater curtain by the summer mold and saltpeter fungus. For the length of this "set," the sidewalk is raised, providentially forming a kind of stage, and all who passed by it were, for better or worse, transformed into "characters," amplified like an echo, projected on the comic or the imaginary. I said to myself: it is my fatigue. I closed my eyes a moment. When I reopened them, it continued to happen, like a story told in a foreign language with too many characters. I went to look at the wall more closely: the surface was a beautiful velvety material, like that of an old pot pulled from the oven. Between the holes and some vague graffiti, a childish hand had written *baka* (stupid). I took it to refer to me: I had passed by it a hundred times before noticing it. But it was not what I was interested in. Just across the way, between the tramline and the street, a garbage dump, with crates and boxes, furnishes a comfortable observatory, where I can see without being seen. I returned to my room at top speed—two and a half miles—then went to Shinjuku to sell my last books to buy film. I found an entire lot, marked half price. "Fell in salt water," the merchant said. We will see.

... That is where I live for four days, hanging like a tick in front of my wall theater. Settled on a box, the camera on my lap, I watch the Azabu quarter walk by, unaware of me. Courtyard side, garden side, the view is clear. I survey those who approach; I calculate their speed and trajectory; I cross my fingers that they will pass in front of my curtain, that they will greet each other or, better yet, make faces. But no one grimaces in Japan.

I even have company: three junkmen with broken teeth and potbellies who spend the day like field mice in garbage heaps. They are at the foot of the work before me, where the garbage collectors dump the tipcart each morning: two old men and one old woman with gray skin and loose teeth. In the afternoon, with sweat on their foreheads, leaning against the piles that cook slowly, fermenting, they read from fragments of magazines, wrestling newspapers, comics, torn from the garbage, pages stuck together with fruit peelings or sprinkled with watermelon seeds. All three wear steel-rim glasses (no doubt found in one of the tipcarts) that strain rather than aid their reading. Sometimes the woman spits on her glasses and cleans them with a piece of her shirt, in the hopes of seeing more clearly, while her old companions tease, tickle, and joke with her. These are the *eta*, these ancient outcasts whose lives the Meiji restoration tried to better. They continue to share the lowest jobs with the Koreans. The world debases them, and I have the impression that these three surrender easily. They are interested in my enterprise; it's a kind of vengeance for them, and they giggle each time one of the passersby is "seen" without seeing them. Around five o'clock, they line up in the Ueno metro to sell what they gather here, and sleep I don't know where.

Then I have the wall to myself. The light is most beautiful at this hour. When the wind blows from the north, the smell of sausages from Rhineland, the Bavarian restaurant, comes down from Kasumichō to tickle my nostrils. When I am stir-crazy, I go down to the discount bookstore, one hundred yards south of my wall, where I have found, among the magazines, the worst of de Sade and Restif, in pirated English editions printed in Taiwan. Standing, reading, I flush with a good shot of glowing obscenities, then I return to my wall. When I am hungry, I always find a few perfectly edible tomatoes in the peelings forgotten by my colleagues, and note that the Japanese are right when they accuse the *eta* of being negligent.

This evening I have finished my last roll of film. Fortunately. In four days, I was becoming a mythomaniac. The simple passersby weren't good enough anymore. Before my wall, I wanted some action, a quarrel, an assassination . . . the emperor.

I climbed slowly toward my quarter and my room. To the west, a haze of light floated over Shinjuku. Araki-cho is silent. I can hear the water drip at the deserted *sento,* which two girls are leaving, combing their hair. I look at the torn posters on the fences: Rikidosan, the Korean wrestler who is the idol of Japan this year; *Nekrasov,* playing in Shinjuku; and a warning against fires: *Kaji wa haji* (A fire in your home is a disgrace). Not ruin, disgrace. And Nero did it for glory!

The coalman is seated on his doorstep, a napkin around his head. His fat face melted this summer. In the morning paper he read an article three columns long, "Why don't we have squirrels in Tokyo?" They have cicadas instead. Ten days ago, Mushiya-san, the insect merchant, came through with his cart and everyone bought a creature housed in a small wicker cage. Every night, at the most secret hour, a chirp arises, thin and solitary, then a hundred, then thousands, until at last the whole quarter hums like a huge field of wheat. That reminds me of an old refrain still sung in the Kansai:

> *Kiri-giri sua*
> *Khane de naku ka-ayo . . .*
> *Semi hara de naku . . .*

> *The cricket cries with its wings.*
> *The cicada cries with its chest,*
> *but me, more sensible,*
> *I come to cry on your stomach.*

Here, during the summer, life is thin and meager like the strong but used fabric of old clothes; and then there are instances of unforgettable sweetness, perhaps because they are paid for so dearly. And it is not reasonable to ask for more . . .

I sold my wall theater to a Tokyo magazine. First two editors looked over the photos, perplexed. Then four, then eight, then sixteen. They had also, over the years, passed by it without seeing it. That is what one misses by always taking a taxi or a tram.

This earned me almost half of a ticket to Europe, as well as a letter from a sick student in a city hospital, which ended with this (I am respecting his japanglish): "From childhood I have been dreaming a big, fat, nice trip like yours. But anyway, it was only a dream . . ." Three one-hundred-yen bills were pinned to the bottom of the page; underneath them: "This is very small money, please buy the ink and paper for your task. Excuse me the letter of no consequence. I hope your big success." (Signed: K. Morohashi)

INTERLUDE

I bought the paper and the ink, and eight years later, I returned. But with my wife and child. In 1964, the Year of the Dragon. The country, the memories I had: all were changed. Nothing fit together anymore. Everything had started again. The vitamin boom had replaced the culture boom: whole families were injecting vials; the workers were in a state of collapse, the blood too enriched by these improvised products.

They have closed the "houses" and the peasants in short skirts of Shinjuku-ni-chome have returned for good to their rice fields and their turnips. Shoji, the barman-poet who had lent me the tables of his café for my first night in Tokyo, was the associate director of a plastics business and worked on his golf.

No one speaks japanglish, only "good" English, and the cops practice their syntax for the *orimpiku* (Olympics). For the Olympiads they have resurfaced *my wall,* like new: the old one seemed too messy.

Rikidosan, the wrestling idol whose portrait was plastered everywhere, was dead, at the height of a stunning career as a gangster, stabbed in the restroom of a nightclub he owned. Two ministers in office had followed the coffin of this friend, so useful. When police and thieves start to send laurels to each other, it is a sure sign that a society has recovered its audacity. It seems that only the emperor, the flag, the sumo tournaments, and the smell of the toilets have not changed. There was not a trace of the agitated, disorderly, and hot Tokyo that had seduced me.

I went to settle in Kyoto.

PART THREE

---•---

THE PAVILION
OF THE
AUSPICIOUS CLOUD,
1964

THE TEMPLE OF
GREAT VIRTUE

———————◆———————

AT NIGHT, with their expanses of streetlights and neon, most Japanese towns look like great cities. Then day comes, and they are no more than collections of buildings hastily crammed under a festoon of electric lines, insulators, and extinguished neon signs. The visitor feels as if he has been tricked.

Not in Kyoto. Despite the slow and singing dialect that sounds provincial, and the multitude of small shops and family businesses, it is still the Imperial City—planned and built by the magistrates, strategists, astrologers, and gardeners of thirteen centuries ago, in an immense quadrilateral that follows China's example and does not skimp on the proportions. With its grid of avenues and alleys, its wealth of temples, cemeteries, rock gardens, of moss and azaleas, its markets, and its artisans, it is the only city in Japan that seems to have an interior space and a concerted plan. The only city where the walker can see the axes—the cardinal points that geomancy considered so important in times past—and the subtle influence they exert on the allure and the ambience of the city. "Walk ten minutes to the north, four to the northwest, and from there, it's about a hundred yards south": this is how the people of Kyoto (who all have a compass in their heads) give you directions.

Kyoto is protected from typhoons by a string of hills on three sides. A subsoil without clefts spares it from most earthquakes. The intervention of an old American consul saved it from B-29 bombs. Kyoto would easily be placed on my list of the ten cities of the world worth the effort of living in for a while.

Like Florence or Ispahan, it is also, unfortunately, one of those cities of art that is almost exhausted by its artistic abundance: where you can't find a beam that wasn't sculpted or decorated by a famous artist, nor a paving stone where two famous warriors were not slain; where there is such a concentrated "cultural density" that you are too busy knowing, discriminating, and learning to have any time to feel; and where you are surrounded by such fine connoisseurs that you are induced to work even harder. A city of specialists and critics, where a bland academic respect too often replaces freshness, Kyoto, well aware of its weaknesses, has coined an excellent proverb about itself: "Throw a stone in the air, you will hit a professor."

The foreigner, whether from Osaka, Tokyo, or Denver, is tolerated as an unfortunate necessity here: tourist livestock allowed to graze hastily before being herded back to the train station. To avoid social exchanges (which they dread), the inhabitants of Kyoto who speak a few words of a foreign language take care not to show it.

It is not easy to find lodging.

MAY 1964, IN THE NORTHEAST QUARTER

By a stroke of luck I managed to rent a building within the huge walls of the Buddhist temple of Daitoku-ji. Translated literally, our address is "Pavilion of the Auspicious Cloud, Temple of Great Virtue, Quarter of the Purple Prairie, North Sector, Kyoto."

> *Up above not a tile to cover the head*
> *down below not a crumb of earth to stand on*

Since the days when it defined itself in these terms, Zen Buddhism has been enriched: never in all my travels have I been lodged more grandly than here. The wall of the Temple of Great Virtue couldn't fit onto the Champs-de-Mars in Paris, and it would take many long lives to count all the tiles on the rooftops. The Daitoku-ji (the name of this temple) is one of two sources of the Rinzai sect of Japanese Zen Buddhism and governs a hundred temples issuing from this line, across the country. It is an immense complex surrounded by adobe walls; it has three monumental Chinese-style doors; a *hondō* (main temple); a *sodo* (monastery); a belfry with a pointed roof that shelters a bronze bell whose vibrations regulate the schedules of monastery life; and finally, a score of subsidiary temples, each nestled between its own cemetery and garden, each preserving its individual ambience, its traditions, its faithful, its intrigues—often with "drawn fans." Within these secret walls, there is a network of alleys paved with gray stone slabs. Scent of pine trees. Soaring foliage, stiff and alive with cicadas. In a cemetery, a priest in a raspberry robe recites the sutras on a tomb, and it is like the sound of a distant fountain. The smell of resin; unseen children crying *chi-chi* (papa) somewhere in this labyrinth; then waves of lofty silence. The dancing silhouette of the deliveryman from a Chinese bistro on a squeaky bicycle. Two monks pass, greet each other with low bows, and go on, keeping their thoughts to themselves. One is a saint, the other a scoundrel, and they both know what they are: this is true courtesy. Here, there is not a gesture or a word that hasn't had its slightest consequence weighed in advance. Behind this austere peace, one senses springs wound tight, and under this dulled and dried politeness, a vigilance that is seldom allowed to slip.

In the ceremonial hall behind the third door, a thirty-three-foot-tall golden wood Buddha smiles to see his faithful maneuver so adroitly and walk so carefully on eggs that don't exist.

In the exact center of the enclosure: the Pavilion of the Auspicious Cloud.

In fact, behind its massive door, the pavilion is a great temple that could easily house twenty; it stood a generation ago in the countryside in the north of Japan. The Daitoku-ji, which inherited the building, had it taken apart piece by piece, moved, and then reconstructed in this garden full of bamboo, citrus trees, and white butterflies. Then, no one had known exactly what to do with it; after a lot of wheeling and dealing, the "Auspicious Cloud" became part of the Ryosen-an temple, which rented it to a Western sinologist, who in turn sublet it to me for five months (complete with servants, a notebook of duties, and an infinite amount of prudent advice starting with this: do anything you want... except make a "bad impression").

The frame, newly reconstructed, had not yet recovered the play that would let it absorb earthquakes, and the weakest tremors rattle the roof with a series of dull rumbles.

"You will see, *dannansan* (master)," the gardener said to me, "the night it wakes you, it is like a tiger bounding along the roof."

He is a man of about fifty, with cunning, yellowish eyes in a smooth face: I feel on my guard around him. While he gently weeds his grass, he is observing us: counting the empty beer bottles and reporting all that he finds suspicious (orgies, depredations, negligences, etc.) to the monk of the neighboring temple, who has designs on this pavilion. Someone said to me: "He is Zuio-in's man." As for the cleaning woman who comes by each morning to wash the wood hallways, polished like silk, she is well established in *hondō* (the principal temple) and probably combs through our wastepaper baskets. Just like in the novels of Walter Scott where a knight cannot pass without someone murmuring: "Prince Jean's man... the duke of York's too." We are also responsible for a gigantic red tomcat, very neurasthenic, who claws and bites if he doesn't receive his daily thrashing. No one knows for whom he's spying; his perverse temperament is forgiven because of the skill with which he traps and kills the huge, poisonous *mukade* (*Scolopendra japonica*) that hide in the roof beams, sometimes tumbling down on us while we're sleeping—their bite makes a person swell up like a pumpkin and is purulent for a good two weeks. Lastly, hidden in the wardrobe, our worst enemy: The Machine. It is an old all-copper robot with levers and thermostats, linked by underground cables to the principal buildings of the enclosure; at the least suspected heat, it sets off a deafening noise in our temple, and an alarm signals the neighboring firehouse. When the weather is too hot, the machine goes off continually and our enclosure, ordinarily so calm, is invaded: red cars, ambulances, cops, bells, sirens descend from all sides and stop, tires squealing, at our door; firemen jump to the ground, put their hoses in firing position—a veritable attack.

When they are finally convinced that there is not the least bit of smoke and that nothing is burning anywhere, the assault softens. They start to refold their equipment, sit on the running boards of their cars and laugh, embarrassed—but they can't get the idea out of their heads that, one way or another, it was the foreigners who broke the alarm.

With all this nearby, we are at home, and it is wonderful.

> *Stop worrying*
> *And follow the flow*
> *If your thoughts are connected*
> *They lose their freshness*
> SENG-T'SAN

"What merit have I acquired by spreading the Good Law?" asked the affable emperor Wu, great protector of Buddhism, of the monk Bodhidharma, founder of Zen in China.

"Not the slightest," responded the patriarch.

"What then is the first principle of the sacred doctrine?"

"Nothing: nothing is sacred."

"Then who are you to present yourself before Us?"

"I do not know!"

The emperor must have suspected that such rudeness from a saint was concealing something worth a closer look, but he was content to show him the door and sink into puzzlement.

About a thousand years later, Francis Xavier landed at Kagoshima and was received very kindly by the priests of the Zen temple that dominated the city. He was shown around the monks' quarters and the *zendo* (the meditation room), where the novices were seated in the lotus position, their eyes fixed three paces in front of them, absolutely immobile.

To his question, "But what are they doing?" his friend, the priest Ninjitsu, replied, "Some are figuring how much they received from the faithful last month, others are asking themselves what it would take to be better fed and better dressed, still others are thinking about what they are going to do in their spare time—in short, none of them are thinking about anything at all sensible."

An absolutely honest response. Francis Xavier should have asked himself whether such triviality in people whose character he admired didn't hide something important. He wasn't prudent enough to do this and was content to note that the Zen monks were formidable adversaries in discussion and that, despite their lively and open spirit, there was no way to convert a single one of them.

These are two kinds of answers to the question "What is Zen?" The first is the deliberately boorish answer; the second, the platitude so conventional that our Western spirit, so taken with categories, asks how the devil it can possibly be the tiniest bit "sacred." And if you ask a Zen monk you have befriended about this point, you will probably receive a good whack on the shoulder as your only explanation.

Being neither monk, nor patriarch, nor even amateur Zen meditator, I cannot approach this question from any of these points of view. So let me explain a little. Contrary to an all too common opinion, Zen is not a "detached" phenomenon, a simple entity that can be discussed in isolation, like black humor or bullfighting. Zen is one of the lessons Asia drew from Buddhism, and whatever liberties it was able to take later, it stayed linked to this revelation.

The Japanese term *zen* came from the Chinese *ch'an,* itself a corruption of the Sanskrit word *dhyan,* which signifies "meditation." After having meditated for years, Sakyamuni Buddha "crossed the mirror" and found himself awakened to a world of inexpressible harmony where disputes were reconciled, distinctions abolished—a place where our definitions were not sufficient. He also understood that all living creatures, to be fulfilled, should and could reach this illumination. All his life, he preached meditation and awakening. He said further that no one can rekindle a dead fire and that when he disappears, he should be forgotten. Then he died. And they built up the pagodas to honor him, they cut out giant effigies of him, they addressed him in prayers, they started to annotate, philosophize, and quibble over his doctrine, on the Twelve Causes or the Eight Ways—in short, they constructed palaces in the clouds where one could comfortably fall asleep. Meditate and awaken, look within yourself, without letting anything distract you, to find the life you do not see: this is what Zen has retained from Buddhism, and Sakyamuni never said anything more. All the rest—the devotion to images, the hagiography, the study of texts and systems, the speculations, the symbols, etc.—is ultimately no more than a false path, a flourish, a refuge against life, a deception, a bone to gnaw that only delays you, glue for the spirit, missing the obvious. The Buddha speaks of liberation, but if you speak about adoration of the Buddha, you miss the essential. As Zen says later: *It takes only one finger to draw the moon, but those who take the finger for the moon will go straight as an arrow to hell.*

No one knows if there ever was a school of Dhyana in India. But we do know that, between the fifth and sixth centuries A.D., Indian monks peddled these ideas in China and that they were very well received by the Taoists. The Tao (the philosophy of Lao-tzu, sixth century B.C.) also taught that our mind is a troublemaker that interferes between life and us; that we are victims of our categories, and that only a simpleton or a child can perceive the harmony between things and "swim with the current." In the stories of the time, one sometimes encounters Taoist hermits walking through the Chinese countryside, so intoxicated at finding the One everywhere and so oblivious to differences that they pass through rocks without even seeing them, to the amazement of the peasants.

These two mentalities combined to give birth to *ch'an,* the Chinese Zen Buddhism that experienced an impressive flowering under the T'ang dynasty (seventh to tenth century). The hills were covered with monasteries where novices went to learn to liberate their spirits under a master. They were exhausted from the domestic work: cutting wood, gardening, preparing the food and the baths of the monks. They weren't taught anything at all, and they were made to see that their knowledge of the doctrine was ridiculous, since possessing it made them no more able to sort out the simplest circumstances. They were forced to concentrate for hours, without moving or sleeping, on deliberately incongruous riddles (kōan in Japanese) that clearly had no logical solution and made the mind grind its teeth. They had to make daily reports to the master on their progress with their kōan, and all responses to the lesson that were "secondhand" or arrived at by inductive reasoning were met with a good strike of the baton. Little by little, the intellect of the novice was thus flushed out of all its hiding places, stripped of its acquired habits and ruses, deprived of the mirage, so very dangerous under the circumstances, of concepts and words. Soon he had lost his head entirely; he was *a quia,* disappointed, losing sleep . . . until the moment when the accumulated pressure exploded the mental armor like a chestnut shell, and he would find himself set forth in the world (this one here, the same one: his cell), which he seemed to see for the first time "in relief," in the outpouring of marvelous evidence. This is the Awakening—*satori* in Japanese. Once this hurdle is cleared, the solution to the kōan jumps before the eyes, much simpler than expected, or absurd (but this is not important: the kōan is no more than a tool, dispensed with as soon as it has served its purpose)—sometimes a simple gesture, sometimes a whack on the side of the old, venerated master that knocks the breath out of him. The master doesn't castigate but salutes this aggression, with an enormous fit of laughter that signifies: "Thus, you have arrived." And the awakened monk is sent out on the road or taken in as a successor. Henceforth, he can, without danger, employ this purged intellect for any need: calligraphy, poetry, even the studies of the sutras or Buddhist philosophy. He has been vaccinated and is no longer at risk of a swollen head or of "taking a finger for the moon."

At the end of the T'ang era, Zen Buddhism was one of the greatest intellectual forces in China. Its spontaneity and its simplicity rejuvenated all the arts, and China's roads were furrowed by Zen masters who made incredible journeys, baton in hand, to visit and present their mischievous defiance. Japanese Zen painting, much later, made these traveling priests the subject of its folding screens, representing them as a kind of shaggy bumpkin, with a howling gaiety, having an answer for everything, respecting nothing except life, driving Confucius, with his rules and his polite bows, crazy.

Here are some classic kōan: "What is the sound of one hand clapping?" "Where was your 'I' before you were born?" "What is the nature of Buddha?" To this last question, there are many classic responses. I will subject you to two of them: a pound of white linen, a rotten noodle. You can see that the fathers of Chinese Zen were not bound by categories nor by a false respect.

By the thirteenth and fourteenth centuries, Zen was solidly established in the military Japan of the Ashikaga. Taught to a tragic society, curbed by prohibitions and duties, Zen became an art of forgetting in action, a way to refresh, to relax. It was extremely popular among the samurai, who were in particular need of its recipes, but in their hands it seems to have lost a little of its salt, its native freshness. It restyled Confucianism instead of fighting it. In short, it was tamed and made Japanese. Perhaps too much. Nevertheless, it had an impact on every aspect of Japanese culture—the art of gardens, the tea ceremony, flower arranging, pottery, poetry, the Noh theater—a major influence. Even today it provides an absolutely necessary spice to a society that tends to be stiff and formal.

After World War II, Europe and the United States had their turn at the "Zen boom"—a perfectly legitimate infatuation, since a number of Western artists were already unwittingly practicing a sort of Zen, like Mr. Jourdain's prose, and Katherine Mansfield, Paul Cézanne, Henry Miller, Robert Desnos, among them and Paul Eluard (who wrote, "There is another world but it is within this one"), and many others. This craze is in part snobbery too, but that is inevitable, and inoffensive. After the dust settles, among all the books published on the subject, there are about a dozen that are excellent. As for the question "what exactly is Zen?" the most sincere and best-informed commentators (some have spent years in the temples) all have different opinions: for some it is a religion; for others a form of therapy, a means of liberation, a guide to character;

for Daisetz Suzuki (who is to the Zen movement what André Breton is to surrealism), it is a reaction of the Chinese spirit against the Indian spirit. For Arthur Koestler, who attempted to "deflate" Zen in an essay that is brilliant but too hasty, Zen was once an infallible remedy against deadly Confucian formalism but is now no more than a very skillfully maintained deception. (He had come across busy and suspicious priests, through a bad interpreter. Maybe bad priests, I don't know. True saints are not always on hand for writers who are passing through, people who don't need what one knows. In the Orient, knowledge is given spoonful by spoonful to the people who are truly hungry, and the word *secret* means nothing here.) For old H. R. Blyth, who clearly had the best understanding of Japan of any man of his generation (he would be more than a hundred years old today), Zen is quite simply the "most precious treasure of Asia" and "the biggest intellectual force in the world." Moreover, this old gentleman was a humorist who wasn't satisfied with words and who recognized that Zen had not been completely successful among the Japanese.

For me, Zen is simply a house where I happened to be a concierge for four months. Now a concierge certainly is not preoccupied with lofty subjects, but takes care of the mail, hears complaints and gossip (for better or for worse), knows the "rules of the house."

I was interested in other things. I was not going to sit in "lotus," I was not looking for "the profound nature of the Buddha." I took joy in the garden and watched my son grow up chasing butterflies among the tombs in the neighboring cemetery, crying "gentleman" —I don't know why—a visitor must have taught him the word. He was much too small to catch them, but when he was with the butterflies, he was the most Zen of all: he lived, the others were searching to live.

I was not very studious: what I know of Zen today helps me measure exactly how much I don't know, and how sad this lack is. I console myself by remembering that in old Chinese Zen it was traditional to choose the gardener, who knew nothing, to succeed the master, rather than one who knew too much.

So I still have a chance.

THE GRAY NOTEBOOK

―――――●―――――

MIYAMA, KYOTO-FU, 1964

PASSING THE TIME

It is the hottest summer of the century
the hottest day of the summer
the workers with their shaved necks
wave paper fans

At the end of line twenty-three
this morning I learned ten Chinese characters
I climbed into this pink bus
that crosses a mountain pass in the shade of bamboo
traveling the length of the river
walking, swimming, and now:
the sun is a lead weight
the current carries a nibbled fig
the feathers of a chicken killed by a falcon
tree frogs, salamanders, dragonflies
The sky is a gray sponge
three mountains make a round back
On the boundaries of the rice field
it is written that life is smoke
I will make it my own smoke
stretched out in the cool of this cemetery
between Ayabe and Miyama
I have forgotten ten Chinese characters

ZUIUN-KEN, NOVEMBER 1964

The Psalm of the Cricket

1000 crickets
100 crickets
1 cricket

a last born, an obstinate
what . . . what did you say?
How the time passes!

this unsteady song
multiplying the space
of the faded garden
and the anguish
of the death reviving here

PART FOUR

———————•———————

THE VILLAGE
OF THE MOON,
1965

TSUKIMURA

———————•———————

I N TOKYO, in the Ginza metro station, which is the largest in the world, one sometimes sees a small group of ageless men, rustic- and awkward-looking, dressed in rumpled suits, and huddled around a pennant brandished by the boldest among them. It is the village "Association," which has broken into the kitty and come, between sowing and thinning their crops, to see the capital and the sea.

Except for these timid forays, the Japanese peasant isn't seen in the city very much or heard about either. When the rice harvest is especially good, the big newspapers baptize him the "Father of the Homeland," and he makes the front page. This lasts a day or two, then he's back on the third page and one must comb through little items from the back country to find news of him: "A rat charmer made his fortune in the province of Niigata," or: "Eight farmers from Hokkaidō who had planted before the last freeze have committed suicide by drinking pesticide." It's cheaper than gas.

But most of the time, this father is silent, bound to a minuscule plot of earth that he cultivates with infinite care.

Every year, between December and January, the people of the mountainous Aichi province (in central Japan) invite the *kami* of their region to a ritual of dancing and drinking that lasts two full days. It is a celebration, an exorcism, and a complex ceremony of propitiation performed by each village in turn. It is called the Festival of Flowers. Since there aren't any flowers at the time, or any time close by, the name may have been chosen to make the winter seem shorter. Each village has its own spirits. Each spirit has a name, and even a face: a wooden mask with a furious grimace that the dancers take turns carrying. When the last jar of rice alcohol is empty, the last firewood burned, and the last drunk back on his feet, the masks go back into their trunk and the satisfied spirits go back home to order the flow of springs, make the trees grow straight, and fertilize the rice. While the snow lasts, they are the ones who are working.

I saw the Festival of Flowers in the village of Tsukimura. Last year, in mid-December. It is today's cold that makes me think of it. I went with Theo, a Frenchman who was taking photos of the phallic dances for a Paris editor. To each his own. For me, it was more as a way to escape the horrible, pre-Christmas, Tokyo bazaar.

Getting there was quite an ordeal: from Nagoya we took a country train with green velvet upholstery, then the bus, then a kind of shuttle where you ride standing up, hunched over between bunches of turnips and dripping umbrellas. We rode like that to the junction of two valleys and then continued on foot up a dirt road, not much traveled. In an hour of walking: a schoolboy in a black wrap, his cheeks red, his nose running; a badger; a wood-gatherer, shrunken against the cold, carrying a load of dead wood; and a truck full of dried fish whose pungent odor followed us for a long time.

Then the valley widened. It was no more than rounded mountains, one after another, smoke hanging over the frozen rice fields and rotting scarecrows from the autumn harvest anxiously telegraphing the slightest gust of wind. A poor region, austere, contained, as if the earth—reflecting its people—hadn't dared to be very expansive; but the little it had to say was so powerful. Compared to it, even the Auvergne is a parvenu. On the floor of the valley, at the narrow end, is the village. *Tsuki* is the moon; *Tsukimura,* village of the moon. There was still some light on the fields, and the festival had barely begun. The Shinto priest and his acolytes had just gone to "bar the crossroads" to the east and the north of the village, to keep out the demonic forces that come up from the underground. Now they were purifying the dance hall, reciting invocations in great, rumbling voices around a cauldron of boiling water, and clapping their hands to summon the spirits. Across the road, four firemen were polishing an old hand pump made of solid copper and red lacquer, with the excess energy of people who have not denied themselves a few drinks, while a half-dozen roughnecks leaned on their bikes and heaped sarcastic comments on them. We came in for our share of these slightly forced jokes. I had the impression they were trying to be rude and that it wouldn't end there. After a moment, the youngest of the firemen shot up: "Come have a beer with me, you two," and, as he had already been drinking, he took us by the arm and led us to an inappropriate spot.

There was no shop or bistro, just a dilapidated cottage or farmhouse with one room set aside to serve drinks. But that night, since the abomination of exams was approaching, three young girls in black smocks were in the room, on their knees, doing their multiplication tables in front of a textbook.

"The children are studying," said the woman, "and these foreign faces will distract them."

"Three beers," the fireman responded, sitting down on a mat.

I examined him by the light of the bulb: young, clumsily built, with vindictive eyes in a face scarred by smallpox. It was his uniform that gave him so much self-confidence. And it was the first time that he had been drinking with foreigners, and he didn't know exactly what sort of authority we expected from a Japanese fireman. The farm woman grudgingly served us. I could understand it. The whole time that we were there, the girls held their pens in the air and whispered behind their hands the little English phrases that they didn't dare address to us. We left without even finishing our glasses. Night had fallen. There was a crowd around the dance hall, and a few torches were already blazing. We heard a tambourine and flutes, and from behind the lighted windows of the farmhouses other flutes answering. The village took the A-*note*. The fireman stayed planted in the road, swaying a little, a mustache of beer on his lips. We took off, climbing the path up to the Buddhist temple that looks down on the hamlet. He followed us for a moment. It was a hard climb in the dark. We heard him talking to himself, hanging onto the underbrush with two hands, then nothing more. At the summit, a moon, still dim, was rising behind the pines among the pinpoints of stars. The temple was abandoned and poorly decorated. In one corner were the grave-markers of the village dead, three rows of them, freshly painted a bright silver. Here and there, under the "posthumous name," which the family of the deceased obtained from the priest, was a comment: "pious faithful" or "faithful" or simply, for the humblest peasants, "believer."

No one dared to forget his place, even in death: harmony has its price. That is what this ranking of souls is trying to say. At least that is how I took it.

Despite the agrarian reform after the war, peasant society maintains a very rigid hierarchy. The village community resembles a rice field: the sharply defined paddies, terraced on different levels and linked by a system of locks whose function is carefully regulated. A village of forty families can count up to four categories of peasants, who do not have the same freedoms, responsibilities, or rights. Various forms of protection, patronage, and subordination link these categories vertically; and every aspect of these relations is ruled by a very strict method of accounting. Sometimes, even the full details of village "etiquette" are recorded in this ledger, which specifies, for example, who owes a gift to whom, in what circumstances, and for what price. To give a gift at random is to make the recipient *obliged* to you—both senses of the word merge in Japanese—for a claim that had not been acknowledged. Thanks to this niggling protocol, there is an almost complete lack of spontaneity and improvisation—anathema to these peasants who are sticklers and such tired ones. In the drama of the village, everyone, even those with tiny parts, knows his role perfectly, and no one wants to risk public ridicule. And besides, for most people, this dependence is a boon that you don't explain or discuss, but simply seize by whatever end is held out to you.

The countrymen's good humor, Buddhist compassion, the gaiety that is Shinto, and daily contact with the earth and its caprices go a long way toward tempering a rigidity that would otherwise be stifling. The festival also serves as a safety valve, and this evening, after a few drinks, the dissatisfied are able to air their complaints. But only the drunk voices his true feelings in everyday life, people measure their words carefully, and the village is as orderly as a beehive.

The foreigner misled by the festival night will be struck by faces that seem so merry, by glances so much brighter than you'd see in the city, by gnarled bodies dressed in equally rough clothes; and he will probably delude himself and form a naive image of them. But he is the simple one: he cannot distinguish the exceptional from the everyday, the oldest branch from the youngest, those who own the forest from those who are allowed—if their conduct is exemplary—to gather dead wood there, and those who tell others how to vote from those who vote as they are told. He is unaware of the whole strict system governing the communal life: the ranks, debts, and thanks; the "I don't dare" and "I'm not worthy"; the snubs and secret grudges—and this ignorance makes him a perpetual source of trouble. The village where everyone knows his place will not have any rest until this intruder has found one, until he has been "placed" somewhere.

On the way back down from the temple, we ran into the fireman tapping his foot at the end of the path. He had waited so he could take us to eat at his friend's house. He had no idea why we had gone up there. The Buddhist temple was for the dead. He didn't know which sect it belonged to; all he could tell us was that it had burned thirty years ago. A fireman's perspective. What interested him was the *sutoripu* (striptease) in Toyohashi, a country town. He'd never been there, just heard rumors, but apparently, you could even touch . . . He hoped to go see it for his twenty-fifth birthday, with his father.

"He's Swiss, the other's French," the fireman yelled as he pushed through the crowd with us, as if escorting two prisoners. But no one paid any attention. The smell of warm sake and flurries of sparks escaped from the town hall where the first dancers—children from eight to twelve—were putting on their masks while their mothers bundled them up in one cloak after another. Standing at the door, two or three newcomers who looked like city dwellers, in soft jackets and hats, seemed very anxious to make more noise than anyone else. These were the youngest children of a family that lived in the city but came back to Tsukimura for the occasion; they were celebrating wildly, spending money to impress their country cousins. One of them had even paid the taxi that brought him to stay the entire night. The driver, an old man in a fur-lined jacket to whom no one said a word, surveyed this country Sabbath with a hostile eye, a transistor radio hanging from his neck.

NINE AT NIGHT ON A FARM

"They're waiting for us," the fireman tells us, but his "friends" give him a cool welcome. I get the impression they are a rather humble family that the community has burdened with the nuisance of feeding and entertaining us. The grandparents are there, watching with moist, benevolent eyes; the father, whom alcohol renders alternately sentimental and arrogant; and a child of three, sturdy in a new smock, who points and fires his plastic tommy gun at us.

The mats are worn, the paper windowpanes ripped; winter flows into the room, and every word spoken is accompanied by a streamer of vapor. But the television is brand-new, and most striking is another luxury city dwellers would envy if they hadn't forgotten it: space. Under the single lightbulb, hanging from its cord, the festival supper is very carefully laid out: noodles in breadfruit dressing, diced horseradish, cucumbers, bean cakes, raw fish heads, and a bowl of white rice, which a few generations ago was the privilege of the well-to-do.

A poor man's feast, where one must down huge glasses of potato alcohol. Everyone drinks heavily to keep warm, and the fireman has too much. He goes so far as to throw a fistful of coins on the table and is shunned like the plague for his boorishness, taking refuge in a mortified silence with his cap pulled over his eyes. The father also has wind in his sails and says anything he feels like. His eyes popping out of his head, he suddenly cries: "These two Frenchmen have the skin of women—"

"Ninny! Good-for-nothing," the grandmother shoots back, and lands a slap on him from across the table, turning toward us, exposing her gums as she laughs, rocking like a bear cub.

"That's how it is," says the old man, refilling my glass, "during the festival, everyone, people from neighboring villages, all our young people, we are all allowed to be insolent. Even to the richest we can say what we want without respect—even to visitors. It is permitted."

He also explains to me that it isn't rice but wood that brings in money in this village and that the five families that share the forest all have sons studying in Tokyo. That it is entertaining to have foreigners visit his farm. He and his wife are perfectly at ease with us. Their two mischievous faces, darkened, worn like coins, are the only ones I can read, because, at their age, and only at their age, they have rediscovered the freedom and abandon that forms the charm of the old people here.

FROM MIDNIGHT TO TWO IN THE MORNING

The spirits—now it's the adolescents, naked legs in straw sandals— carry heavy wooden axes and dance around a fire that's spitting sparks. A party of villagers, towels knotted around their heads and torches in hand, surrounds them, answering them with a kind of slow stamping.

"Are they all good Devils, your spirits?"

"Very good, all excellent!" the Shinto priest tells me, shivering.

He says it with genuine affection, but during the next dance, the spirits are nevertheless knocked around, sprayed with fire-brands, and noisily pushed out into the night. After their avataric performance, the spirits return through the back door, and I see two of them arguing about a motorbike through their masks, try-ing to hit each other, but they can't manage it, because they cannot keep from dancing. The music has moved into their legs. It's a seven-note tune in which only the rhythm varies, a tune played by a drum and a huge bamboo flute, which is answered by other flutes

(pulled from every pocket) in the room and in the night. The air is filled with this insidious song, with steam, with ice and fire, and the smell of alcohol is strong enough to make a horse drunk. All those who aren't drinking are made to drink, and I observe that the conversations around me are all bogged down in drunken repetitions. Each person has found a small morsel of truth in the bottom of his glass and is teaching it, relentlessly, to his cronies, none of whom are listening. Me, I'm just about at the end of my vocabulary: there isn't a word that I haven't used three times. I could extricate myself with a laugh or with mimicry, but for that I would need to understand the gestures! Here, a raised thumb means four, the fingers fanned out flat means that one is drinking, and a confused swing of the chin can very easily announce a punch in the mouth. It's no more than crude horseplay, with a quick give-and-take, but everything's said too fast in this performance. Though his profession makes him a fair mime, my companion, Theo, won't venture any further than I with his grimaces. He asked everywhere about his phallic dance, trying to find out when it would take place. One person smacked him on the shoulder; one emptied a big glass over him; one replied cheerfully with a hundred obscene jokes; but no one gave him an answer. It wasn't that they were at all embarrassed or the least bit furtive about it, but after a few jugs of sake, the village really didn't know what to make of these strangers with their eyes turning everywhere. Our curiosity put them a little on their guard. That phallic dance—if there is such a thing—it's possible that they postponed it until the next day. Out of a kind of economy. In the process of trying to understand, there is always an element of taking, and this village has nothing to spare.

TWO OR THREE IN THE MORNING

Deep in the woodshed where I had taken refuge to pull the film from my opened camera, I tripped over a couple of lovers and got knocked on the head with boards as they fled into the darkness. I should have expected something: two in the morning is the hour of the bull in their astrology. One of the animals of the Chinese zodiac, the bull governs bold enterprises and secret meetings. But all the same: to flirt in this cold, on these planks full of splinters!

"*Gomen . . . gomen*" (I beg your pardon) cries the man as he runs away in great clumsy jumps.

But look, I'm the one who is sorry. Unfortunately, I didn't see the girl, who disappeared first, proving the saying, "A pulled-up skirt moves faster than a pair of lowered pants."

There are now two huge fires burning; the firemen feed them, staggering wildly. If they let the fire spread in some places, it is the women who put it out. The villagers are sitting in a circle around the fires, hands held out toward the flames. As I walk past them, an old man shouts, "The Swiss . . . the Swiss," and gets halfway up as if he is going to speak, but then sits back down. I hear his wife tell him: "To shout at him, without rhyme or reason . . . Once you've started, you should tell him something."

But he stayed there, staring at the fire with a guilty look. I laughed when, after I'd gone no more than fifty yards, he caught up with me, struck by the idea that he might have offended me. He touched my elbow and gave me a smile that displayed three teeth, a warm, sincere smile. And not in the name of his village or country, no. It was truly his own smile. Charming, since after all I am the troublemaker. Sometimes I ask myself what makes the old people so much better than everyone else in Japan. Perhaps it is that once they are sixty, society loosens its grip enough for them to regain their humor, and then the kindness natural to the Japanese flows freely.

Together we return to the town hall. Along the road, a long line of peasants are holding onto each other's shoulders and pissing in the rice field, politely reminding each other not to fall in.

FOUR IN THE MORNING, AT THE THIRD FARM

A gray man grabs me by the shoulder: Come to my house . . . Yes! You must!

It is the city man who kept the taxi. He is shaking from alcohol and the cold, and I have the feeling that his elegance garnered him a few jibes that he has not yet digested. Clinging to me like a lifesaver, he crosses the road, goes through a door, and deposits me in the midst of a family at their table—that is, kneeling around a low table—without saying a word. And the women, who are sober and composed in every situation, push to make room for me and bustle around serving me, giving us reproachful looks. But the *kimochi* (the good atmosphere)—more vital than oxygen to the Japanese—is quickly restored when a child, sleeping behind the table, wakes up, sees me, and clasps his mother round the neck, crying with fear. Between sobs, he points to the door, crying: *"Baka kaere yo!"* (Go home, you idiot!)

No one is too worried, since a three-year-old always has a right to show anger, but after a while these cries seem infernal. I know exactly what I should do: sing him a little song, show him a Chinese shadow puppet—in short, quiet this bawling with the petty seductions and amusements used here. But I am too cold—there's nothing like the cold to make a person unfair—and besides, since five in the afternoon I have done nothing but smile, bow, and be sociable.

"That's my son, that's my son," repeats the man in the suit, as if it were something to boast about.

Then he goes rummaging in a sideboard to have me smell the perfume that his brother-in-law brought his wife from France. Chanel No. 5. He holds it up to the light like a piece of the True Cross while the pretty urban wife and her peasant sisters-in-law in blue cotton breeches murmur "Paris... Paris." It took all of my efforts to keep them from spraying it on me. To distract them from that notion, I returned to the subject of Paris. They knew many things from television, but wanted to know what the shops were like and if the different trades were still grouped like they used to be in the Tokyo of long ago. We started with the Cadet market, a spot that I know well, and the wild boars carved up and sold there, and then came down toward rue Richelieu. The mounds of food on rue Cadet, the Armenian bakery, the smoke shop, the betting booth—I described them all. Then the "Queen of Preserves" (founded in the eighteenth century), rue du Faubourg-Montmartre, the all-night oyster bars, the bookstores in the Jouffroy arcade, where Léautaud stole some books. When we got to the National Library, they asked me: "Do you like Japan?"

FIVE IN THE MORNING

One should not dismiss Japanese music until one has been subjected to it for at least six or seven hours. At first, in the afternoon, I hadn't been much impressed by this flute tune because of its slowness and hesitating rhythm, which took a long time to get established. But by midnight, I felt I had grown into this melody. Now I am music drunk, and as time goes by and the flutists take their turns (playing right now is a peasant who wears two jackets, one on top of the other), the music becomes stronger, more menacing. It has turned into a drunken refrain, smoky, quivering. The torches of the dancers flicker and sparks fall, showering necks numb from the cold. Their faces are drawn, cheeks sag, their eyes are closed or popping out of their heads. It is as if the difference between face and mask has diminished, and everywhere I see beaks, jaws, and snouts.

Here and there, since it is permitted, a brief blaze of malevolence still flares up, someone explodes at the top of his lungs— but it doesn't last long. The music carries everything along in its larger rhythm. When a dancer collapses, another takes his place. Fatigue, drunkenness, a trancelike state take the village back in time, to the black centuries when taxes left so little for people to live on that one out of every three newborn babies was suffocated. Now, the dancing is no longer a diversion, it is a rite. The hamlet forms a solid block that excludes all foreigners. The villagers don't see us at all. The taxi driver too is in quarantine. He hasn't had much success moving around the crowd with a photo of a nude woman, hoping to strike up a conversation. In his desperation, he tries it out on me: a dyed redhead, sitting on a beach. A model, he tells me, that he hired for an afternoon with fifteen of his colleagues.

She is very beautiful, and so are the waves. Poor old man; shouldn't have to drive a taxi at his age.

At dawn, the spirits will dance down to the village below. I could not watch any more of it. I was too cold, I had drunk too much without being able to get warm, I was too hungry and I had spent too long waiting. I needed to escape from the smoke, from the drum, to walk in this winter night. But not on an empty stomach. A while ago, I had discovered an old man secretly simmering almost fifty gallons of soup over a wood fire in a lean-to behind the town hall. I went back to his shack. He was dozing, sitting on a pile of sticks, waking up to stir his pot with two hands, to throw in a handful of dried fish, and then going back to sleep. The smell of his broth made me almost swoon. I complimented him and he thanked me very politely. But when I held out my bowl, his eyes grew cold and he suddenly stopped seeing and hearing me. This is not for you, this soup: it must go to the right people, in the right order, at the right time. And how should he know what this clod with his dirty tow-hair was doing here? But on the other hand, saying no is not polite. So he extricates himself from this difficulty by dismissing me mentally—a tour de force, since his hideout was small and I was talking louder and louder. I can still see this old Tartuffe quite clearly, standing at his post behind the enormous cauldron, staring unblinkingly at a spot just below my mouth and transforming me into no more than a puff of steam. That is the formula here: when faced with the unseemly or the unexpected, look just to the side of or beyond it. This convention— which is universal here—always allows for the probability that it's nobody's business. By the time I carefully took the ladle from him to refill my bowl, the old man didn't see me anymore. He had fallen back to sleep with a shadow of a smile. This worked out well for both of us. Throughout the whole business, I had been wrong and he'd been right.

SIX IN THE MORNING

The frozen dirt of the road rings underfoot. The white frost and a biting black sky give the valley that finishing touch—a ray of moonlight, fog in the right spot—which the Japanese countryside always needs to be at its best. Above the whiskery pines the constellation of Taurus is very clear. We walk quickly, and I feel the warmth coming back into my bones. Ten more miles to the inn. I ask myself how many stones we will have to throw at the door before it will open, and whether it will be cheap. I still have this damned flute song in my head, and when I look for words to get rid of it, these lines of Rutebeuf come back to me from afar:

> *Pauvre sens et pauvre mémoire*
> *M'a Dieu donné, le Roi de Gloire*
> *Et pauvres rente*
> *Et froid au cul quand bise vente.*

> *(Lousy sense and a lousy memory*
> *God gave me, the King of Glory*
> *And a lousy living*
> *And ice on my ass when the north wind's blowing.)*

That fit pretty well, to the music and the moment. The last verse certainly. And the French is exquisite.

When we had reached Hogo, light was whitening the rice fields, making the turnips hanging on the front of the farmhouses shine like mother-of-pearl. All of Japan is still under its eiderdown.

PART FIVE

THE ISLAND WITHOUT MEMORY, 1965 – 1970

THE ROUTE
TO THE NORTH SEA

———————●———————

At the fairground shop
three pennies' worth of haze
is all that I saw
through their telescope.
KOBAYASHI ISSA
(1763–1827)

Man's mission
on earth is
to remember
HENRY MILLER

HOKKAIDŌ IS THE northernmost island of the Japanese
archipelago and the second largest: a little more than twice
the size of Switzerland, with five million inhabitants. Rice fields in
the south; volcanoes, pasture land, and forests in the center; and
to the east, a sea full of fish, one of the richest in the world. From
December to April, snow covers the island, and the ports on the
northeast side (at the same latitude as Milan!) are iced in. Hokkaidō
(*hoku:* north, *kai:* sea, *dō:* route) means "route to the north sea."

When August comes and exams are over, when millions of ven-
tilators and fans are making a futile effort to cut the simmering
heat of Tokyo, a heat that has silenced even the pet crickets in their
little bamboo cages, the Japanese students climb into packed
trains and head north to get some fresh air and receive their "space
cure" on the island of Hokkaidō. Tent stakes, compasses, maps at
1 / 100,000 scale, and boxes of dried raisins: that is the "Hokkaidō-
rush." And it is new, because before the war, except for botanists,

ornithologists, lighthouse guards, and people sent there by their companies, no one went to Hokkaidō for pleasure. In fact, it was the last place in the world an educated Japanese would think of visiting.

Hokkaidō fills an odd place in the mental geography of Japan. Most Japanese in their forties have not gone there and will never go there and don't think much of it. This island has no prestige in their eyes because it has almost no history, but you have to realize that they never cared enough about it to give it one: barely having discovered it, they turned their backs on it, and this neglect has lasted for a thousand years.

In the year 658, Abe no Hirafu, a Japanese captain in the campaign against the Ainu (who still occupy the northern part of the main island), armed a junk and went up to Sakhalin and crossed the straits of Soya; on his return trip, he established an "imperial office" in the wilds of southern Hokkaidō that was never heard from again. Then he hurried back to the court on the Yamato plain, to "return to his classes" there. At this time, in fact, Nara had not yet been built; the imperial residence moved every time a lord died, and all the "important" people (the upper-class people) were craving the Chinese fashion, eager to learn the ideograms, to read horoscopes and the calligraphy of the sutras. Buddhism was in full bloom. In the northernmost part of Hondō (the present Tōhoku), a few energetic and ambitious barons were carving out immense fiefdoms, secretly clearing the land, and getting rich, but the imperial officers appointed to keep watch over these lands just fretted about how unpleasant they were. In the eighth century, the letters they wrote to the court were all sighs and laments: that they were not in Kyoto alongside the Kamogawa, with good friends, commenting on the cuckoo's song and composing bits of verse in rather pedantic Chinese. They were mortified colonists in a province of weeds, briars, and wind, disturbed by a nature too coarse to bend to the delicate lines of T'ang paintings or to aesthetic gardening. Even the moon, the axis of all sensibility, was frozen and shrunken in these expanses, no longer the huge familiar lantern to which a person so readily confides. To say nothing of the long winters, for

which the Japanese knew no other remedy than hot baths, alcohol, and, finally, spring.

Such is the image of the northern part of the Great Island at the end of the twelfth century: a land of violence and snow, without saints or calligraphy, where one only goes in exile or disgrace. This image hardly changes at all. As for Hokkaidō, which was then called Yezogashima (the island of the barbarian), it was still no more than the almost mythical, boreal Tatary that was barely mentioned in the chronicles of the time. Its first visitor of note happened to be a ghost: the famous Yoshitsune (the greatest mercenary soldier of military Japan and hero of innumerable novels and plays) who in 1189 was killed with his family in a fortress full of traitors, and whose legend was passed on to Yezo, where the Ainu added him to their primitive pantheon. Close on the heels of this shade came the remnants of the great Fujiwara clan; beaten and stripped of their land by the central government, the family took refuge there, settling modestly at the southernmost point on the island. These exiles built military posts here and there, traded with the barbarians, and sometimes relieved their boredom by repressing a citizen's revolt or decorating their beaches with a line of severed heads—all the while staring south to where history was being made in their absence while they waited for a reversal of fortune. Or for visitors: mostly fugitives like themselves, plus a collection of adventurers, phony priests, people with a pack and a rope—true pioneers—who went up into the forest, clearing, trading with the Ainu, breeding with them, digging open-pit mines, and living on the sale of furs and semiprecious stones—a trade profitable enough to warrant contact with China, via Nagasaki, right under the nose of the central power. This went on for centuries, and no one today would know any of this obscure history if Japanese television hadn't gone there and gotten hold of it, to teach young people about these "Leatherstockings" and "Mohicans."

But the fishermen have known about this area longer than the cartographers, especially Russian fishermen. In the eighteenth century, Russians were firmly established in eastern Siberia and their whalers started to clean out the straits of Tatar, the straits of Soya, and the coasts of Yezogashima. They tried to obtain the right for their boats to dock and take on water in the islands' excellent harbors. When their emissaries went to the Hakodate anchorage, they were captured by the Japanese government, who read them an edict sentencing them to death, offered them a huge drink of sake, and sent them back unharmed—without responding to their requests. The government in Edo (Tokyo) was worried by these foreign incursions and finally sent a priest-mathematician to make a map of this territory, which had concerned it so little previously. In Japan, a name is inextricably linked to fortune: after failing an exam or losing a tournament, the student or professional wrestler changes his name and starts over. At the end of the nineteenth century, Yezogashima did the same. The island of the barbarians was rebaptized Route to the North Sea (Hokkaidō), which increased its prestige a little, and the extraordinary team running the new Meiji government went to work on it. The country was changing rapidly, experiencing a burst of energy that would turn it into a great modern power in a single generation. Hokkaidō was declared a strategic territory and went on to play a major role in the government's plans for industrialization. Mines, fisheries, factories, and paper mills were built there with funds from the public treasury, which absorbed development costs for ten deficit years before selling these businesses to private companies for almost nothing in 1881. Boatloads of settlers were given free transportation to military settlements: a few boneheads went for the adventure, but mostly it was the poor, driven off their small farms by need and not very happy about it, and the *eta*, who hoped they could escape their origins in this exile. Gunners for the coastal batteries, technicians, petty gangsters who controlled a lot of business in the city of Hondō, and teachers. And missionaries: American Protestants, French Catholics, and members of "new religions" that sprang up in the Buddhist revival—Hokkaidō's new settlers, still confused and lacking traditional references, were like putty in their hands. In 1871 a new capital was built in Sapporo, laid out in a grid, while a Yankee agricultural engineer (lent to Japan by President Grant) taught the settlers large-scale farming and the construction of "American-style" farms—square houses with sloping red-tile roofs, flanked by round silos—that contribute to the charm and interest of the Hokkaidō countryside.

Hokkaidō had a new look, but that wasn't enough to overcome the mistrust of the mainland Japanese. Too many unfamiliar ingredients had combined in the mixture for them to recognize their own style in it. They were still not sure if Hokkaidō was in Japan. Until the last world war, when a series of bad harvests uprooted the peasants of Honshū, they still preferred to settle in Brazil, where they were surrounded by businesses started by Japanese immigrants and could scarcely tell they had left home. Even today, most of the time, a young assistant professor from Tokyo with an appointment to the University of Sapporo will rent a tiny room there like a soldier in a garrison, leaving his family in the south, convinced that on this island without a past, they would lose their refinement and become *mannu-nuki* (straightforward, lacking manners), a term the Japanese borrowed from the Americans (*manu* means manners; *nuki* makes it negative) and sometimes applied to them.

And now, let's end the lecture . . . all the trains for the north leave from Tokyo's immense Ueno station. It's nice, this station: inside it's like a huge hive, black with soot, formed of long, poorly lit galleries where young men with sideburns hold out placards that read *Konban o hima nara, denwa o kudasai* (Alone tonight? Deign to call) with a six-digit number. Others, more furtive, peddle stolen merchandise. The produce merchants in scarves and blue cotton breeches lug huge sacks of cabbage and turnips on their backs.

Across from the station there is a wide boulevard where the noise, the light, the movement are reminiscent of the Place de Clichy during rush hour. Under a web of electrical lines so tight it blocks the sun, there are dusty plane trees, fast-food restaurants, and stands with chestnut vendors; there are palm readers, licensed tooth-pullers, and shabby cinemas with eight-foot-tall cardboard cutouts showing the stars of the movie with severed heads flying, naked women in chains, huge laughing faces. Under these distorted images—which turn out to be false, found nowhere in the film—is the crush, slow and tired, of elbows, shoulders, backs with sleeping children hanging from them. There's a huge stairway that runs from the boulevard to a park; beside it, two veterans, "war cripples," sing, "play the accordion," and pass the hat. They are always at their post here: their white tunics and prosthetics are part of the landscape. These are fake soldiers—last year the veterans' association had the last of the real ones retire from a profession they considered shameful—but they are truly mutilated and they only utter the melancholy cries used in the Philippines or the Malaysian campaign to make their injuries more real. Beyond these two tin soldiers stretches the long park; I go there to kill the hour before my train leaves.

What can a person do in a park? Parks don't seem real to me. I am bored stiff, then I remember the adage of Lao-tzu: "The journey of a thousand miles starts with a single step." I start to jot down notes: *zuihitsu* (thoughts without coherence, at the tip of the brush), the way the Japanese so willingly do—they have never believed in rigorous sequences nor in demonstrations to prove that . . .

AT THE MATSUSHIMA INN

In the Japanese mind, the West is a muddy being, loaded with lumps of slag. This definitely describes me this evening. Also, the perfection of this unadorned bedroom oppresses me. Reproaches me. Makes me feel as if I'm dirty even though I have just bathed. As if I have too much hair, and immodest desires, and maybe one or two extra limbs. In this style of decor—as in the food—there is an immateriality repeated again and again: make yourself small, don't hurt the air, don't wound our eyes with your terrible colored shirts, don't be so restless, and don't offend this slightly bloodless perfection that we have been tending for eight hundred years.

I understand it perfectly, but the country and the summer have already sucked me dry like a raw egg and there's nothing left but the shell, and I don't see what else I can do or how I can further reduce my existence. Matsushima, in the province of Sendai, is one of the Three Landscapes of Japan. When the monk-poet Bashō

arrived here three hundred years ago, he was so overwhelmed by
what he saw—this still-wild bay, these dozens of bald islands in
the mirror of the sea, with perhaps a little mist to soften the
unbearably vast horizon of the sea—that the poem he wrote to
describe it says simply:

> *Matsushima yah!*
> *Matsushima yah!*
> *Matsushima yah . . .*

This poem is softly sung a little on a receding half-tone and surely
could not be improved upon: there are some cases that call for
repetition, and Asians understand this better than we do. This cry,
the echo of a cry, then the echo of an echo fading away—and it
is unclear if the man or the landscape has disappeared. And it's
so beautiful—this lesson in impermanence that the pilgrim mur-
murs to himself as he stands on the shore, where there are still
only two or three mangy innkeepers and a few capsized boats
covered with barnacles. Fifty years ago, to judge from the old,
primitive sign I saw above the pastry shop, this place still had a
certain charm.

But today, it is the "Matsushima Yen"! It is Sylvie Vartan on the
loudspeaker on top of the little Zen temple. Tourist barges that
roar and stink. (We introduced all this schlock, and it has been
passionately embraced.) Matsushima is tourists lined up behind
numbered posts, waiting for the *drive through the country* like fidget-
ing children in line for the restroom. It is little live crabs—live
ones sell better—placed in plastic shells. It is boxed lunches of rice,
opened simultaneously, with a sharp rap, at the order from a kind
of responsible supervisor. Fortunately, night finally falls, and the
whole world, this world that deserves so much better, goes to
sleep. Fortunately, the light of dawn is beautiful, and the tourist is
not an early riser (beer is heavy), so there is half an hour at least
between the first rays of sun and the first train from Sendai, and
during that time you can still tiptoe to see *"Matsushima yah!"*

NOHEJI (NORTH HONSHŪ)

The sun has risen over this little train station, fields of rain-rotted stubble, the rich green fields that go straight from my eye to my stomach. A grass full of *clover,* a grass that I had not seen for almost two years, and only one night on the train and two degrees of latitude north and I find it. I get off at a station cluttered with square trunks and covered with a sweet-smelling rug of sawdust, and I arrive at this poor village's only street, where each of the villagers carries a heavy hoe on his shoulder, where even the children are ageless, where so many details say "the north," satisfying something in me that has long been unfulfilled. These are: weeping willows; double daisies; intensely colored wash on a background of wet grass; a blacksmith surrounded by the smell of scorched hooves; a saddlery where harnesses are dyed deafening colors; and black horses set everywhere like weights securing the landscape, which save it from the unworldliness (is it still a landscape?) of this collection of southern "views" so appreciated by connoisseurs, huge horses who don't give a damn about Zen, weighing three hundred kilos—they all drag you down like the "squawk" of a contrabass, and are completely swallowed up by the same clover that makes my mouth water.

AOMORI KEN (IN THE BUS)

Last year, 1964, for the first time, the Japanese could easily obtain passports and foreign currency and take their vacations in foreign countries. Many of them took advantage of this. But Hawaii is expensive, Hong Kong is far away, they are not very welcome in Manila. Shanghai, they won't consider going there yet. As for Nakhodka, on the Siberian coast, it isn't a very cheerful spot. Also, when the month of August comes, there are always twenty million Japanese traveling around Japan. The travel agencies, the *Wandervogel* clubs, the societies for the improvement of young people, etc., have cut up the country like a cake, without leaving a crumb to spare, and the portions are so small! Even the destinations that are only third- and fourth-rate are busy twenty-four hours a day taking care of their thousands of tourists. Even in the most rural districts, the bus driver has learned her speeches of praise by heart as well as a few lines of local folklore, which she sings into her microphone each time she sees a "knapsack" pointing. But usually, the man with the knapsack (it is me) is dozing because he has just been, say, standing for ten hours in a train that was crammed to the rafters; and so all this knowledge is dispensed to a few peasants who go about their business, since they've known these songs since childhood (with the correct intonations, which is difficult), and don't really listen but applaud politely anyway.

But me, the bus driver doesn't let me miss anything. "On your left, a wild hydrangea... this hill is six hundred yards and the other twenty-two at least..." I should take notes: that would make her happy.

THE GRAY NOTEBOOK

———————●———————

RAIL JUNCTION

What can one see here?
The bears, the brothel, and the station
murmur voices under umbrellas
And just as it was in the Wild West
the big event is still the train
everywhere high axles rusting under giant umbels
and the locomotives with their bronze bells
blur this child's black-and-white drawing

Between heaps of bog two students
play cards next to a puddle
they have to travel through this summer
which is like autumn elsewhere
The farmland, the green fields lying fallow repeat:
"one . . . two . . . three hundred crows . . . "

Say! this place looks like it was made with the remains
from the ruins of other less godforsaken landscapes
but what it has that's unique
what touches me
what no neglect can take away
is this thick Norman cloak of grass
and on it these black horses
which nod their heads madly "yes" at me,
full of hope and ideas

Leaning at the train window
where a hundred thousand elbows
have made the wood shine like silk
I think of my rough life and when my heart aches
I look at these black horses
anchored in the fields like heavy ships
and their horse-nature does me good.

OSHIAMAMBE, 1965

THE AINU

---●---

A VILLAGE NEXT TO a volcano will never know hunger: all it
has to do is dam up the nearest hot spring and open an *onsen*
(thermal bath). Throughout history, there have always been thousands of *onsen* in Japan, always crammed full of radiant bathers.
There's one for each illness. Some claim to cure everything. At
others, in the mountains, peasants spend the coldest part of the
winter in water literally up to their necks, with a rock on their
knees to keep them from toppling over when they fall asleep.

After a careful soaping and rinsing, you plunge into the *onsen*
pool and stay there for hours. Entirely naked, of course, since it
makes no sense to wear clothes in the water unless you are
deformed. Men and women are not separated, but that doesn't
excite anyone: at the *onsen*, the ablutions are what matter. Since the
Westerners came, troubling or troubled, there's a little less candor,
and the Japanese have started to play a silly game: first covering the
stomach, then the breasts, with a tiny towel.

Other foreigners will say to you: "Ah! the *onsen* . . . the mas-
seuses . . ." Their eyes turn wanton, and their smiles get round as
buttocks. As for massage, it is the same thing; but there are two
kinds of massage. On the one hand, there is an ancestral art perfected
by the Chinese and Japanese and usually performed by the blind.
On the other, of course, "massage" is an instant alibi that covers for
the most basic acts; for this, less of an apprenticeship is required.

At Noboribetsu, the largest *onsen* in Japan, I spotted a *Massages*
sign, and I asked to have one, to try it. It took four phone calls to

the concierge, a half-hour wait . . . and in comes an old woman who could have been a nun, her legs covered with black veins. She has a handsome face, worn and luminous, like the face of a blind person. But she can see, and she leads me up the dizzying stairs to a closet that is her room. There is a cast-iron stove, a mattress covered with a clean sheet, a reproduction of a Dufy, and an old man she's just finished, who is lying there sighing, a towel knotted around his head. I take off my clothes; she has me lie down on my side and starts with my neck. She closes her eyes while she works so that her fingers, which are hard as boxwood, can communicate clearly. From time to time, her hands fall on a knot, on a pain I didn't know I had, in a part of my body that is not very lived in. So she searches it out, roughs it up, dislodges it, and it is as painful as a visit to the dentist. She works down to my toes, then she attacks the other side. I look at the waxy face behind the closed eyes, peaceful, working, and ask myself if, forty years ago, she too was one of the "sweet young things" that people tut-tut about. Maybe, like the toads in fairy tales, she would turn into a lascivious young princess. Maybe there is an open sesame, a magic word I could say, but it is not in my Japanese vocabulary. And besides I would have lost the naturalness her ugliness gives me, and here that is a much rarer commodity than sex appeal. When she is finished, my whole body tingles, loosened all the way to my fingertips. I feel as if I have rediscovered the innumerable ins and outs of my body, like a hundred-room hotel under my skin.

NOBORIBETSU (AT THE STATION)

In August, groups of Japanese young people go to see the wild west of Hokkaidō, on split-second schedules with barely enough time to go from train to bus and from that bus to another train, where some of them diligently read descriptions of the countryside. The train compartments are packed with young bullies and girls glowing with health; these two camps observe one another but rarely speak despite their desire to do so. Then, when some little devil, egged on by his companions, suddenly decides to ask his neighbors where they are from and where they are going, the whole car follows his game with interest. So what should naturally become smiles, jibes, and awkward remarks that affect them more than the most polished maneuvers gets stuck stewing in brains that are already stuffed with exams. The girls get pimples or grow melancholy. Occasionally (but rarely) they commit suicide. The boys become extremely timid or secretly violent; finally, one day, they may gang up six-to-one to teach a lesson to a riled friend, beating him so viciously that he never gets up again. These playground battles that turn into murder are not uncommon; I have found a half dozen in this summer's papers.

People go up to Hokkaidō because it is cool, but also to experience the "solitude" much touted by the travel agencies. But you can never be alone there: wherever you go you find fifteen or twenty people, with a few radios as well. Solitude? Fine! As long as it is numerous. Of course the lower price of group travel plays a considerable role in this, but there is also the sheer pleasure in plenty of company. I have no quarrel with that: these students are simply less misanthropic than I.

Here and there, you see a black sheep, a person traveling alone—yes, all alone—but whatever warm feelings that inspires disappear when he lowers his head to confess that he's alone, as if he had a shameful disease.

The loner who came up alongside me is a boy from Osaka. His buddy had let him down, or had gotten sick. He has been alone for twenty-four hours. He has visited a restaurant, two craters, the edge of an "officially listed" forest, and he's homesick. He consulted a timetable to see if he could hook up with me.

"Do you like Japan?"

In the right mood, yes, very much. But I don't like that question.

"Do you eat sashimi? . . . Do you know how to walk in *geta* (wooden sandals)? . . . eat with chopsticks?"

This anxious questioning, so common it's become pathetic. The answer to all the questions is *yes*, since raw fish *is* an exquisite food, the *geta* have their advantages, and about the superiority of two polished-wood chopsticks that are used only once over a stainless steel fork that goes from mouth to mouth, that's pretty obvious. Living "Japanese-style" doesn't present any problems, it's a pleasure in fact: just boy-scout training, as a young French father put it so aptly. It is living with them that is sometimes a bit prickly . . . *and simply living.*

My visitor notices a book on the table and absent-mindedly leafs through it. A grimace tugs at the left corner of his mouth, and I can see that it's not going well. I should help, I shouldn't hesitate. But I can see that he is looking for a teacher . . . and I had really hated school. Besides, I know so little worth teaching. So I reversed the roles; he taught me the rules of *shogi* (Japanese chess). I soon became drowsy, leaving him to the solitude that he must learn to deal with at some point. And which I am myself gradually mastering.

In the country, the peasants often asked me: was my mother still alive? When they learned that she lived on the other side of the earth, a real compassion filled their faces: what! All alone in a rice field, surrounded by strangers, so far from his village and *from his mother* . . . "At least," they sometimes added to comfort me, "when she writes to you, you get pretty stamps."

SHIRAOI

In the Ainu language, *ainu* means "man." (There—that beginning at least has the merit of simplicity.) The Ainu are of Caucasian stock, natives of central Asia, who occupied the largest part of the Nippon archipelago at the time that the present Japanese race (Yamato), composed of very diverse elements, came to settle there. The Ainu were hunters and fishermen; their culture never reached the agricultural stage, they never acquired written expression, and their language, which is unlike any other, is—like Basque—a headache for linguists. The Ainu are also the hairiest race on earth and are said to be little concerned with cleanliness. From the beginning, the Japanese seem to have experienced an irrational revulsion against the Ainu and never spoke of them except in pejorative terms: *emishi, ebisu, yesojin* (barbarians, primitives, yokels). Certain Japanese psychiatrists find "horror of hair" to be one of the reasons the Honshū colonies made so little effort to settle in Hokkaidō. At the time of Nara, the Ainu held all of the Great Island north of the Sendai-Niigata line and wouldn't let anyone dislodge them. The Japanese sent generals against them (great calligraphy but feeble strategies) who ended up sending official letters to the court to justify their retreats. Then, under assault by more hardened captains and pressure from a civilization a thousand years more advanced than their own, the Ainu slowly pulled back toward the north, hotly pursued by the Japanese, who gained ground with each new dynasty. In the seventeenth century, the last Ainu were firmly established south of Hokkaidō, squatting on the last hunting grounds of a culture that, like the native Americans', would soon disappear completely.

THE EARTHENWARE POT AND THE COOKING POT

From reports made at the time in Nagasaki by the Westphalian Kaempfer, the Japanese did not have the highest opinion of their new subjects:

Robust, with long beards and hair, they are as adept at archery as at fishing, and feed themselves exclusively on fish. They also maintain themselves very coarsely, being dirty and smelly, but (he adds) *one cannot put too much faith in that, the Japanese being so very enamored with cleanliness and so fussy about their ablutions that they have even accused us of exactly the same thing.*

It is true that the Dutch, like all foreigners, were reputed, probably for good reason, to smell like rotting meat; one popular joke even claimed that when the *komos* (redheads) went on a trip to Kyoto, all of Kyūshū's flies followed them there.

While the flies were so busy, the "war of the barbarians" flared up sporadically in the north, whenever there was an Ainu uprising.

One last rebellion in 1789—then the Ainu merged, without any more fuss, into the thin stream of Japanese colonists. A census in 1945 showed a population of forty thousand; another, in 1962, sixteen thousand. Today the "Ainu reserves"—three huts over here, a row of straw shacks over there—are kept up for the tourists' satisfaction. The tourists are very disappointed, but they won't admit it, because what's the point of ruining a vacation that you can't take again?

In the village of Shiraoi, near Noboribetsu, there is an Ainu settlement of a few families: you can get a better look at it apparently. I went there. As you enter the burg, there is a cracked panel with a picture of an Ainu woman in costume, her face decorated with a half-moon tattoo that covers her mouth, making her smile whether she likes it or not. Turn left under this painting and you come to a dirt alley bordered by handicraft shops where Ainu in official costume sell products made of leather, wood, fur, mangy remains of a magnificent art, hastily produced and fragile, like objects not made to be used.

When I arrived, it was raining heavily; the tourists were staying away. The Ainu had not had many customers that day and I received a good welcome. Business was already winding down and half the traders had swapped their colored tunics and their birch-bark crowns for raincoats and baseball caps. Three snotty-nosed children (reinforcements can be produced in case of a flurry of business), squatting in a truck tire, are playing a game (Ainu, no doubt), a game I still haven't been able to figure out. Under the eaves, the men quickly whittle wooden bears; two young girls, who could have found better uses for their beauty, polish the bears with a brush.

"I make fifteen or sixteen a day and with that I get by," one of these Stakhanovites said to me. "Would you like one?"

But it was expensive. I told him that I come from a country full of wooden bears, that there are even bears on flags. He called two old men to come to his aid; they tried to tempt me with another bear, half price, a little damaged, with wheedling, flattery, pleas, in an amusing, whorish style. Then they gave up; they would sell

it tomorrow morning to someone half-asleep. Of all their carvings, these bears sell best—the only things that are truly hideous and not at all Ainu: the universal bear knickknack, exorcised like the mask of Beethoven.

I walked around this tiny quarter watching night fall on the closing shops. I was disoriented: Ainu... Ainu... where are the Ainu on this dilapidated stage set? Maybe this is all there is—this crap and the sweetness in these fleshy faces, the eyes shot with bile, where you find the same mixture of weakness and contempt that you see in the eyes of bums. There was still a little light, and I took several portraits of the shop owners. They were amused to see me there with my camera equipment and muddy shoes, come from so far and working so hard. I remembered the Brassens refrain: "With my little bike I look like a jerk, my friend..." They let me do my work for a minute and then explained to me that the real, the official Ainu—the ones with handsome beards, who posed for a small fee most of the time—were already gone and that it would take a tour bus with a guide, at least, to make them come back. All the same, through the window of an Ainu straw hut, right in the middle of the sheet-metal shacks, like a diorama in a colonial exhibition, I came upon one of those photographic stars: an old woman bent by age singing as she swept her small, dusty museum. She thought that her day was over, but she was wrong. Someone had to pay for my long trip in the rain and for this whole farce I'd found at the end of it. I had her pose five long minutes under the only light bulb in her hut, and she stood there—erect, resigned, mechanical. Arms awkwardly folded in front of her, telling me a string of sad stories in a thin voice as she waited for me to leave. Usually, her visitors photographed themselves standing next to her, using an automatic timer, and then, good-bye. She couldn't understand why it took me so long. But she let me shoot her portrait, and this woman—chestnut color, features almost erased by age, a marriage tattoo giving her the large, sad grin of a clown—I couldn't tear myself away. Now I was the one who didn't want to leave. When I told her how beautiful I found her, she put her hands to her head with a flirtatious little laugh, like the laugh of a schoolgirl. She told me that if I came back the next day I could see the men. She even insisted I return, tapping the back of my hand, and so redeemed my baseness a little.

I came back. I saw them. Both of them. Each occupying his post in a narrow space, dug in, awaiting customers. Like two competing smoke shops on a little-traveled street. The first one was already wearing his rig, grumpy; he looked like a druid in an operetta, with his crown falling over his eyebrows, holding his sword like a spoon. I offered him cigarettes, but what he wanted was fifty yen. He said to me, *"Suwanai . . . nomanai"* (I don't drink or smoke). No doubt the travel bureau stuffed him with these virtuous lies, since the Ainu are notorious drunks and inveterate smokers. The other one, across the way, is much better. I recommend him to you: an admirable broad beard and the head of Gaston Bachelard. He carries his eighty-eight years lightly and loafs on a lounge chair in tennis shoes and beach pants, sending smoke rings toward the sky. Now here's one, I said to myself, who keeps up with the times. Not only that, but if he's dressed this way it's not because he has grown lax; rather he has preserved his pride and only puts on his traditional clothes when the spirit moves him or when circumstances dictate (and he's the best judge of that). Proud, malicious, he makes fun of all the common people parading past his door.

"What annoys me," he told me, "are all their questions, because I've forgotten almost everything."

He went to fix tea for me. He is the cousin of the old woman I liked so much.

I don't regret having put myself out to see them: these two old men are, after all, the last chiefs of a nation that used to occupy half of the archipelago. And besides, they share with M. Eisaku Sato, prime minister, the distinction of being the three most photographed people in Japan. It is true, and probably in a less transitory way.

Poor prey caught in the trap of mechanized society . . . weak and powerless victims, I can resign myself to understanding the destiny that is annihilating you, but never to be taken in by this witchcraft, so much more feeble than

your own, which holds up before an eager audience photo-album substitutes
for your destroyed masks . . . (Claude Lévi-Strauss)

The second Ainu settlement is located a few miles east of
Shiraoi, along the shores of a lake fringed with reeds. There are
three traditional straw huts and a long line of cement stalls where
the Ainu sell souvenirs, everything from fur hides to decorative
uniform braid, to "Ainu" pillboxes and cigarette-holders shaped
like phalluses. Not to mention the bears, of course. Most of the
arcades are in the hands of young *Ainoko* (Japanese half-breeds)
who own other businesses in the city and come and go between
their businesses on brand-new Honda motor scooters, wearing rubber boots and blue twill suits. It's the new wave, assimilated, who
almost speak only Japanese. In Ainu, "I owe you thirty-nine
francs" is said as "I owe you nine, plus two times twenty, less one
times ten." It is the most complicated system of numeration in the
world, only conceivable for people who possess just a few objects
at any one time. It's easy to understand why the *Ainoko* have
strayed from the flock. Even more since their trade in trinkets is
doing so well. In Shiraoi—that miserable village—they even have
a sophisticated little jazz club where they go at night, after leaving
the baths, to drink beer and listen to Thelonious Monk. I spent a
wonderful evening there with the son of the innkeeper, a lumber-
jack, a champion speed skater (the loudmouth of the group, who
kept putting in and taking out the false teeth he wore after each
outburst), and the bartender in a white shirt (he drove a truck during the day), who lit our cigarettes with a solid gold Dunhill and
told me that he spends his free time translating Hemingway into
Japanese. All equally open in spirit, direct and uncomplicated.

Almost all the pure Ainu belong to the older generation; they
are primarily for show, extras who throw on their costumes in the
cabin of the bus when they hear that a group of tourists or scholars
is about to arrive. Then they sit in quiet groups on the shore of
their lake while they wait for the photographers to finish. For an
extra charge, they bring out two black bears that are playful
enough to do a few tricks (I can't really call it a dance).

I arrived in the middle of one of their displays. The costumes—
white or brown tunics decorated with curvilinear motifs, primarily
black, green, and red—were wonderful. The faces, sullen: it's not
really a life, constantly reenacting "what used to be." Japanese
tourists, following their guide, were already at work: the field full
of cameras, light glinting off of lenses. I went to the center of the
circle and started taking pictures, raising cries of *"Gaijin ... kankei
nai"* (This foreigner in here . . . that's not right). Literally: *kankei*
(the relationship) that would give him the right to do this does not
exist. I had been careful to crouch, to stay out of their pictures, but
maybe the unforeseen presence of a foreigner at this spectacle robs
it of the last bit of authenticity it had.

Of course "foreigner" is an ambiguous concept, and it's easy to
reverse its sign; usually they take it upon themselves to shower him
with special favors, which are not always spontaneous, so that he
may take away "a good impression"; but all it takes is for him to
be dusty, or droopy, or step outside the proper *kankei* and he opens
himself to a barrage of secret resentments and frustrations that can
go on forever. There's no need to be alarmed, it passes, and anyway
it's perfectly natural. So when you take pictures, there are days
when you shouldn't worry too much about being popular, just go
about your work. That came out well, thank you.

I left around noon, walking toward Samani. A mixture of rain
and sun. The road, bordered with tall bell-shaped flowers, pastures, the occasional farmhouse with a red tile roof, runs like an
arrow toward the horizon. A little steam train, a picture-book
train, is trailing a puff of black smoke over the sleepy countryside.
I zigzag along this wide road, saying hello to the horses now and
again, kicking a tin can like a man in a Fellini film, and dreaming
a melancholy dream about this culture of bear hunters and trout
fishermen, about the freshness of their language of fur, birch, and
clay, about how few of them have survived.

"For thirty yen per person," the official Japanese guidebook (1962
edition) states precisely, *"the friendly, gracious Ainu are willing to
show visitors their cultural heritage, their treasures, their homes . . ."*

Ainu, Wahines, Ouled Naïls, Hopi and Navajo of America:

poor children corrupted by Thomas Cook! Here, in fact, it's as if twenty Gauls had been preserved on a reservation at Gergovie, with their hatchets, their bloodshot eyes, and their crab lice. Not even enough to write a thesis on, and God knows they make them pretty skimpy today!

If you ever pass through Shiraoi, be sure to go to the jazz club: a year from now, they'll know enough English to tell you what Hokkaidō could become some day.

A BEE STING ON A FACE IN TEARS
(Japanese proverb)

I left Shiraoi in the late afternoon. The sky was overcast: I felt like walking and decided to go back to Noboribetsu by way of the beach. I crossed the marsh that lies between the sea and the road and came to long black sand dunes threaded with bone-colored roots. Not a soul, not the trace of a footprint. Here and there, a deep double track made by a seal, and patches of fog that were moving as fast as a bus. I took off my shoes and dug my toes in the sand, listening to the frozen cries of the seagulls and the crashing of invisible waves. I had twelve miles of beach to myself; I said "the sea... the sea" over and over again and I was content. The simplest pleasures are the best. An hour later, night crashed down on me and I found my way blocked by a channel the sea had cut to a lagoon. Bending down, I could see a strong current riffling the surface, but I didn't want to go back the way I'd come—the idea of crossing the marsh in the dark didn't appeal to me. I put my clothes in my bag, the bag on my head, and I entered into the channel. It was much deeper than I had thought, and there was a strong tide going out to the open sea. I was afraid to walk on a sea urchin, a piece of broken glass, a sea cucumber. I almost stumbled in the middle, and right then, in a night as black as ink, losing my balance in this strong current, water up to my armpits, I *saw* the friend whom Eliane shelters in my absence leaving our bed—six hundred miles away, stretching out in the most unbearable way. A fool like me, come to live for no good reason in a godforsaken place like this, cannot control this kind of image. Struck by this absurd suspicion, I almost let myself be pulled out like a cork, out the channel to the sea, to join the army of vengeful phantoms that haunts the straits of Tsugaru. Luckily, I quickly regained my footing. To drown with this image in my mind! I, who had always longed for a beautiful death . . .

On the other side, lighting match after match, I was able to find a path that led through the marsh to the road, without going through the quicksand. I was chilled and soaked. I tried to flag down a car with no luck. People were afraid of the darkness and fog, that was natural. But it made me feel a lot younger to shake my fist and shout "bastard" at the taillights of the trucks driving past.

SOUTH OF SAMANI

I was the only passenger on the bus that dropped me off at the end of the line at nine at night. It was completely dark. I was in a tiny godforsaken port where it was raining cats and dogs. I hurried to get to an inn before they closed their wooden shutters. Just in time. They set down a straw mat for me in a room where two other men were sleeping.

Just inside the kitchen door, the owner and his wife were watching television, one of those soap operas where you can tell, from the gloomy way they hold their heads and the fixed expressions on their faces, that there will be many more tears and trials before the lovers are reunited. In one corner of the room, the thirteen-year-old son, who had no interest in this silliness, was shadowboxing, throwing such fierce karate chops at an imaginary enemy that at least half of them would have proved fatal. Feet bare, hair closely cropped, buttoned up in a black school uniform, he was totally absorbed in his activity and breathing hard. His face with its pinched nostrils, the sharp, jerky movements of his elbows, the loud cries that accompanied every hit: it made for a rather frightening performance. You would never see such a thing on a farm in Provence or Vaux, but here you never forget for too long that Japan is a martial culture.

There were 167 acts of violence against teachers committed by primary and secondary, or upper-level, students during this school year . . . A total of 1,695 students were implicated in these crimes . . . According to the same police report, about 17,000 students at all levels are affiliated with criminal organizations all over the country. (From the newspaper *Japan Time*, December 1964)

It's easy to compare the Japanese to the Spartans, and stop there, thinking you've summed it up. The Japanese themselves flirt with this analogy. But it's a bit pat—fortunately, they can also be compared to Athenians or Romans. Running through Japanese history like a filigree there is a taste for the same austere frugality, morose endurance, and masochism that speeded Sparta's plunge into oblivion. Once the dead are buried, one whets one's sword and kills time until there's something better to kill. I'm well aware of the virtues of self-abnegation that counterbalance this national character flaw, but ethics based on holocaust and violence leave me somewhat cold. In the end, Sparta left us nothing but the name of a harsh legislator and a few stories establishing that Spartan mothers prefer to see their sons come back dead on their shields, rather than alive without them. This is obviously just one of many aspects of Japanese civilization, but a major and vital one that has often been dominant since the end of the Heian era. On the melancholy feats of arms that besmirched the Japanese Middle Ages, once again Bashō has the final word. Passing the site of a celebrated slaughter, his pilgrim's sack over his shoulder, he wrote:

> *Natsugusa ya!*
> *tsuwamono-domo ga*
> *yume no ato . . .*

> *The withered summer grass*
> *is truly all that remains*
> *of the dream of the warriors . . .*

It is useless to repeat the fact that these samurai were also aesthetes, connoisseurs of pottery, accomplished calligraphers, or that, like the young Atsumori—a Japanese Lancelot massacred in the flower of his youth—they played the flute to lift your heart; none of that changes a thing. These elevated pastimes, which brought them great honor, shouldn't make you forget that almost all the mental energy of the elite was devoted to the art of slaying and being slain in the service of a lord. Old captains, cast aside by the cruelty of this merciless existence, had no recourse but to shave their heads and take up the robes of a mendicant monk. And they made formidable monks: hardened to pain, always on the move, commanding as much compassion as an army corps. Japanese society is a shackle that one can only escape from the top . . .

The young man has just finished his exercises, and the landlord has closed down his post. I return to my room and sit between my sleeping neighbors, eating a bowl of cold rice. One is dozing, his cheek on a road map. The other is snoring, a greasy hat over his eyes, dreaming of long journeys. His left arm is resting on a huge peddler's box, which has tipped over, spilling out buttons, chewing gum, and razor blades. Rolling out my mattress, I see a flea jump—gone!—no, there it is! No: that is another one, many others. Don't think the Japanese here are less clean than elsewhere, but this is a district of poor people, gripped tight by poverty, and as often as they go to the baths, their fleas join them, then settle into the depths of their straw mats, where it's the devil to get them out. This reminds me of some nights I once spent in a Macedonian inn where the fleas came after me in packs—where I slept anyway, for want of an alternative, with the vermin of the whole quarter, including the mosque. But I should not have stirred up these sunny images—and here I am hit with the real Japanese blues, which start radiating from the stomach . . . and all one's strength dissolves and then evaporates. I don't know of any other country that can slip the chair out from under you so deftly. I need a little hot sake, but I don't want to wake up this sleeping household, and I'm almost out of money. To comfort myself, I turn on my flashlight and reread a few pages of *Jacques le Fataliste,* where they never stop having a good time with their friends and tipping back big mugs of Anjou. I lie down in the dark and, to fight off panic, I tell myself that my two neighbors are Buddhas, and me too: the last *sutras* affirm it.

THE CAPE OF ERIMO

———————•———————

T HE BUS GOES down toward Cape Erimo along a sandy road,
quickly disappearing into a cocoon of fog, and the noise of
the motor is snuffed out like a candle. A dozen of us are inside it,
fighting against sleep, but from time to time a neighbor's head falls
onto your shoulder. During the summer, a constant wind blows a
great blanket of patchy mist, hypnotically white, back and forth
over the cape. It rapidly spreads out and divides up, and through
its rifts you can see incomparably green pastures falling in cas-
cades silent toward the sea. Then all is shrouded once more in
white. Then this green again, with a spot of trembling violet—
wild irises, the petals crushed by the wind that makes their stems
vibrate. On the rocky coast, black rags fastened to poles whip anxiously to signal a wreck, a current, a siren, or god-knows-what sort
of beast.

There is not a soul in this landscape—it is exclusively grass,
light, and eddies: it is poor and obstinate, tirelessly repeating the
same thing, as if in a dream, yes, or in a story told by a wonderfully
gifted storyteller. And when the sun penetrates this saltwater fog,
crisscrossed by wind tunnels where crows fly in odd formation, it
is as if the whole misty and crazy country were held within a magic
crystal ball, and everywhere you feel its rounded surfaces arching
upward rapturously. Immense pastures, immense talent. I ask myself
how the bus driver can cross this glass palace every day without
falling into a sort of intoxication or hopeless melancholy, how he
can still think of the clutch or the packages to be delivered.

And it is good, this bus. No fixed stops: here, a woman gets on; there, two children get off and disappear into the opaqueness, holding each other's hand. The bus hums calmly in the wind and moves across this royal velvet landscape like a beetle going about his business. Plus, a bus is the perfect vehicle to enjoy this spectacle: you wouldn't want a horse here (too romantic and so you'd feel the same); nor would you want your own car (dealing out slaps to your brats who are blocking the rear window); nor even a horse-drawn carriage (it's picturesque and full of enticing accessories so you look at the copper lanterns and the mare's ears and exclaim "This carriage, God, what luck!" and its charm will seduce you and get between you and the scenery).

But in this bus nothing distracts me. I have taken it so often. It is all familiar to me: the driver's seat belt, which is too tight and makes her stomach stick out; the sharp breaths she takes to help with a maneuver, *orai . . . orai . . .* (someone's passing); the plastic rose in a vase above the driver's head; the microphone that hums a little, which she taps in vain trying to silence it; the passengers who look like torture victims in their sleep. I know these things so well, I don't even see them anymore. Intimate, reassuring. It is like being in the belly of one's mother, just a bit bumpier . . . Besides, the bus isn't expensive (I paid four francs for an all-day trip), and that's for going everywhere. Sometimes even through a ravine, into a river, along the bottom of a cliff lapped by waves, and all the packages float away . . . then it's good-bye life or, worse still, good-bye to women or, if it's your head that takes a knock, good-bye to the tricky math problems and clever quotations dropped at just the right moment. But if this misfortune did befall you, if you couldn't distinguish the yin from the yang or the Son from the Sainted Spirit, you could expect a general sympathy. There is no longer anything to be feared from a wounded foreigner. The district hospital will bend over backwards for you; the stretcher bearers will fold origami hummingbirds and whales trying to raise a smile; between two injections, you will be visited by a local journalist— an ex-officer of the Imperial Navy maybe—who won't know how to work his flash and won't tell you anything about the trials that drove him to this modest position, although you can imagine the worst, since the pathetic and the everyday often go together here. Then someone will show you the article about you in the local paper (*"Tragic destiny of a foreign visitor"*); on your bed will be letters (not one, but seven, or eleven) from schoolgirls—sad, sincere, passionate. And the nearest professor will come over on his motor scooter to translate them for you: "I am alone on the farm, I think of your mother. The cherry trees have already flowered; the plum trees not yet. Think of your ancestors, of the seasons, and you will regain your courage." In short: such wonderful letters—young Werther never wrote their like, and you will never receive their like again...

... A pothole bumps me awake. I must have been dreaming a little between yawns. The sun is higher now, and it is even more beautiful. The bus has stopped before a crimson mailbox. There is a small settlement here: five houses whose sheet-metal roofs painted turquoise, red, and blue float in this luminous mist, and along a half-moon-shaped beach, five boats decorated with mysterious red designs that look like runes. Rising above the boats and the roofs is a steep knob of a hill covered with the same perfect green velvet that I had seen this morning, and precisely at the top, a huge black horse tearing at the grazed grass with abandon. There isn't time to ask if he climbed up there by himself or if he ever gets dizzy before he is swallowed by the fog. It is as if Hieronymus Bosch had outdone himself and then an even more masterful painter had worked over the painting to rid it of the little rocks, devilries, everything unnecessary. For years, without knowing it, I have been waiting for these images, which move me in some unknown way. I get off the bus and stand by the side of the road, I feel almost drunk, my head is buzzing, I have trouble swallowing, like someone who has unexpectedly been granted too much. I continue my journey on foot.

ELEVEN IN THE MORNING

Again, a mailbox, boats, and houses in the same wonderful arrangement: solid houses made of washed-up boards that no longer have anything to fear from the sea. Through the window of one of these cabins, I can see a couple and I watch these fishers for a moment as they cover their drying rack with seaweed several feet long and thick as a fist. I have not yet encountered many people on this coast, but the ones I have seen have been couples, and never very far from each other. Just like the albatross with its plovers. The wife is generally a little fatter and her curiosity makes her bolder. I knock on the windowpane.

"Hello!"

"Come in!"

"Is it impossible to take your picture?" (It is more polite to word the question negatively, and the simpler the life, the more this politeness, which embellishes it a little, is justified.)

"Certainly not!" (That means: Yes, if you please . . .)

She has come out into the light, on the threshold, and I take her portrait in an "American salon" style. Then the man cuts some seaweed into thin strips like chewing tobacco and fills my pockets with it. It is *kombu*, which is ordinarily eaten mashed with vinegar, and it seems to be the only resource these villages have.

I go my way, chewing on this leathery thing that contains all the tastes of the sea: salt, iodine, hints of a school of anchovies or the oily wake of a cargo ship. Turning it over on my tongue, I even think I can feel the pulse of the tides and the pull of the moon. This takes the place of lunch.

VILLAGE OF ERIMO, NOON

All the faces here have half grins and a worn look from the constant wind, but in the creamery, across from the bus stop, I see a girl made up like an actress, who is cramming old crates into a small, Russian stove. I go to sit down near the stove, which is lit year-round, and she brings me some milk. She has eyes of a gray-violet color I have never seen before in Japan, and moves with an easy grace that is startling. I find her very beautiful in the intense way people have here. And what can she be doing in this out-of-the-way corner with perfect makeup and polished nails? For some time she has been running the household of an uncle who woke up a widower one morning. But before that? She trained sea lions with a traveling show in the port of Muroran, and she goes back every Sunday to work with them a little, because those little animals, you know, they forget faster than we do. Good! Since she already has violet eyes, why wouldn't she train sea lions too? And after this the whole morning seems good to me.

Occasionally a face emerges from the fog, presses itself against the creamery window, and examines me carefully. They come and go: sometimes, I see two or three at different heights. It's because the people of this village don't have many visitors: the bus comes once a day, and every once in a while there's a shipwreck, or a weather airplane gets lost and crashes in this fabulous fog. Only here, today, have I understood what I was looking for on this island.

BETWEEN KUSHIRO AND ?
(FIVE IN THE MORNING)

This local train is packed with old men in breeches and old women in kerchiefs struggling, in the half-light, to wedge tin cases between their seats, where they bounce at each pothole, oozing and spreading a horrible stench of low tide. These are the peddlers who are going to the far ends of the country to sell the scraps they gathered this morning in the port: codfish heads, pieces of octopus, small crabs that are a bit damaged. The shabby riffraff of the fish world and it stinks, since even in the sea, the poor have their smell. The women also carry red and green candies, which they wrap up in cellophane in packages of five and which, despite all the care that they take, end up smelling of herring. Crouched in their seats, they work at full speed, nonstop, without any chatter, but once in a while they give their neighbors a quick punch in the calf, which makes them collapse in laughter and livens things up.

The two old women across from me have finished their work, pulled out their *bento* (lunchbox), and are eating their breakfast—

sticky rice and a few shreds of sour cabbage—literally on my knees. Then the first unfolds an immaculate handkerchief and, with a gracious gesture, wipes the grains that have spilled on my cardigan, while the second strikes a sulphur match and lets it burn down to her fingers because she has let fly with one of those winds not considered good manners.

Now the rising sun reflects off the marshes and fills the car with a beautiful tobacco light. Leaden jaws shine, and faces begin to brighten: tanned, wrinkled, their features chipped like cemetery Buddhas; but what is left is very sweet and there is something open and mischievous in their look that I have not often seen here. When you have nothing to lose, you have nothing to hide; and these people, forced to have faith in life itself rather than in their own lives, sometimes fare better than you'd expect. This car may be quite frugal and threadbare, but this is the warmest and most liberated company that I have encountered in Japan. I don't say this out of a sentimentality like Richepin's, but because I can see how readily these people help one another, how well they get along, how easily they find things to laugh and talk about everywhere. When I photograph them they are amused, without acting embarrassed or silly, because I work so close. They are used to being minuscule in the photographs in their albums, because in those pictures they include as much of the landscape as possible because they consider themselves insignificant.

Now and again, the conversation—a volley of robust obscenities—is interrupted, and everyone moves toward a window to look at the marsh, at a crane preening his feathers, this elegant bird, so inexpressibly white, posed in the middle of the reeds, like a Ming vase.

Sighting a crane brings a thousand years of happiness. A tortoise, ten thousand. As for fish, the deal is not as bad as you'd think: every three years, these fish peddlers who make no more than three hundred francs a month pay a visit to a Buddhist temple, touch their foreheads to the floor and give the monk, in an envelope—folded according to ritual—a little of their little bit of money to pay to hold a service for the repose of the small fry massacred so they can live.

The old Mikimoto did as much for the pearly oysters that made his fortune, and in the Kyoto temples, they hold a service every year for all the needles broken by seamstresses and one for the badgers who gave up their hides so that calligraphers might have brushes. Saint Paul asks: "Does God concern himself over cows?" But the Japanese live in a unified world where one even worries over the mussels . . . after they have been eaten, it's true.

AT MASHŪ-KO LAKE

In France, the guides at historical monuments sometimes go as far as taking off their hats to speak to women (there is an especially courteous one at the palace of Avignon), but a French guide who said to his busload of vacationers "I don't wish to be importunate, but if you deign to turn your head, your eyes will rest on the Villandry chateau" would seem like a bad joke and even risk a chorus of jeers. Here, what they say over the microphone when you arrive in view of Lake Mashū-ko . . . I don't know how to translate it: it is even more polite.

Mashū-ko lake lies in a crater dominated by another crater that resembles a felt hat that has been crushed by a fist. A little like the lakes in the Swiss mountains, but wilder, with the ambiguity a volcano adds to the landscape. In the middle, a small island. No sign of inhabitants, but an observation platform for tourists where, on Sundays in August, you can hear *Osanai de kudasaimase* (Be so good as not to push). There are two other lakes in the area that rival this one, but the Mashū-ko lake is sought out for its "mystical" or mysterious ambience (I think that it is better to understand the word *shimpiteki* in the first sense)—no doubt because some authority in matters of landscape has said so. I am the only foreigner.

"Do you find the lake mystical?" someone asked me.

"I find it very beautiful, but why mystical?"

"Because a very esteemed professor said so—when will you learn to believe?"

"When? Very good question!"

AT THE
ABASHIRI MUSEUM

———————●———————

A S I CROSS the square jumping over puddles, looking for the
local museum, the happy, muddy, runny-nosed children
bring me huge sheets of paper that they want me to sign. We move
under shelter. But I hate signing: giving my name to these unsus-
pecting kids like spare change—this name, which traveling has
emptied of all substance—makes me feel like an impostor. So I
write "scarab," "cavalcade"; I write "farina": in short, words that
contain a bit of music and luck. Seeing me so willing, they call over
other kids, smaller children, who give me pieces of soggy
cardboard, and I sign "Pommard," "Demoiselle of Montrachet,"
"Chantemerle," which is the name of a forest in Vendée where, a
long time ago, I hunted for mushrooms under the same steady
rain. Soon, I see the inn, the bedstead with brass balls on its posters,
the woman who woke up there laughing, and I pause, pen in the
air, caught by the miracle of existence and memory. Sunny clusters
of memory.

"Your names are all different," cries the largest of the group,
comparing the sheets.

She has a rough voice and jumps up and down in the mud,
exposing perfect thighs. The children accompany me to the
museum, where a gust of wind carries them inside in their muddy
galoshes. They drag me from one glass case to another—"Here are
three bears"—and they move on. When I was their age, three
stuffed bears would have kept me fascinated longer, but I suspect
that they come here every day and think of the museum as home.

"Baby crabs." These are small brown eggs peeling in a jar of for-malin. They plant me there and then return to their business. It is early morning and the rooms are poorly lit. It is the kind of museum I like: I feel like I'm exploring the attic of an inventor. It contains:

—an ordinary tandem bicycle painted black, with three posi-tions for the pedals, dated 1911;

—a daimyō sedan chair in black lacquer emblazoned with silver chrysanthemums;

—three birds of paradise from the South Pacific, the gift of a col-onel who was there during the war;

—Ainu sledges and crossbows, which were made without a single piece of iron;

—A scale model of a potassium mine;

—An account book, a travel icon, and a knife with seven blades that belonged to a Russian trader who perished a hundred years ago in a shipwreck off the coast near here.

But best of all, the magical wooden statues carved by an Oroko tribe from Siberia who had come through Sakhalin to settle here. They came with their shaman after the war. Tall as a hand. The face, oval and slightly concave, the nose barely sketched, and little obsidian eyes that follow you anxiously wherever you go. Two of these figurines are standing in a cloud of wood shavings that have peeled from the pedestal and look like they are trying to find their way in a blizzard. One feels an invisible finger placed on all their lips, and so strongly do these dolls express silence, cold, hail, and snow that one instinctively turns up one's jacket collar. Boreal Klee. I want very much to move this entire family to a better light to photograph them, so I need the curator. There he is, followed at a respectful distance by an apprentice in a white shirt. He's a simple old man with a white toupee, who shakes like a leaf from constant excitement. He bows and straightens up with a burst of laughter.

"My dolls have made you cold! Photograph them? Yes! In my office? Good!"

He monkeys with the display case locks, cuts the cords that hold the statues as if each second counts, and picks up an armful of "gods," dropping one and breaking its leg, which is glued back together by the calm assistant. Its slight limp just adds to its mystery.

We place the fetishes on a case covered with a white cloth. The picture-taking lasts three hours, during which the old man never stops his monologue. This museum is his personal collection; he paid the building costs himself, his cellars are overflowing with magnificent objects. Sixty years ago he left Kansaï to settle here and become the patron and protector of the Ainu, then the Oroko and the Giliak tribes, who sought refuge here when the Russians conquered the area south of Sakhalin. He had traveled in Manchuria, Inner Mongolia, and had made a trip through northern China (by bicycle) before World War I; all of southeast Asia in the thirties; ten years ago, Italy, Greece, France, Egypt, Libya; one of these days he wants to visit Afghanistan, the highlands of Bolivia, the Eskimos of Copper Island. Not only that, he is almost eighty years old . . . No doubt his friend the Oroko sorcerer would lend him a flying broomstick. Mr. Yonemura, I would recommend him to you.

I think of the Louvre, that tomb. I tell myself that all museums should be like this one: flowing directly from the arteries of an old man who has a right to its objects, to handle them and love them, make them shine, and, if they get chipped a little by mistake, a skillful factotum repairs them so well that they are more beautiful than before. These museums—you find them in the provinces—are the only ones to provide truly enchanted moments, the only ones where there is still a chance to discover, between the stuffed sables and the Bantu shield, an authentic Stradivarius, or even some pharmacy jars—that seem so fated to be yours that they're enough to transform the most honest man into a thief. The only museums where, thanks to genius and disorder, the past is not arbitrarily cut off from the present. Take the Greuze Museum in Tournus: under the stairs there is a stoneware pot with blue motifs that's easily two hundred years old. One wonders whether Greuze had ground his colors there; no, it belongs to the concierge who puts mashed cherries in it to make brandy.

The photos finally finished, the curator approaches the case.

"Have you seen what's under this?"

He takes the cover by the corner, pulling it with the flourish of a magician as his white toupee spins around. Underneath is a complete human skeleton lying on a bed of sand in the same languorous and thoughtful pose as when it was found near here during a grave-digging. In the eye sockets, the jaw, the crotch, between the humerus and the tibia, sea urchins and colored seashells are nicely arranged.

"You see! The attitude of the body: perfectly natural."

"Yes, but the shells?"

"The shells are for my own amusement."

"Another question: the beautiful tandem bicycle in the first display case, dated 1911?"

"It is mine!"

A DEPRESSION COMING
FROM THE KURILS

———————●———————

M Y TRAIN CARRIES its cargo—sickles, axes with blue blades greased and carefully wrapped in cloth, and sleepers with faces darkened by fatigue—fast and straight through the green night, for the tender grass slopes and fallow fields bordering the primitive forests had gotten so much rain. And now, since the train has stopped, we lean out the window a little: it is a small station in the deep night, full of coils of rope, sacks of sawdust, and darting shadows that move around, uncoiling the ropes and shouting loudly. There are days like this, when no matter where you are, you see nothing but poor people doing poor things, when everyone you talk to seems not to see you, to be counting up to a thousand and waiting for you to vanish, days filthier and smokier than soot . . . I know it, I know it, I still can't get used to it.

For the past twenty-four hours, I have been living on the satisfaction of a huge crab I had the night before last, seasoned with a little vinegar, so fresh I might have been a shark. I have two or three thousand yen left, which is enough to get me across the straits of Tsugaru and back to the Big Island. Maybe my lack of money will enliven this trip a little! Always, except in a brothel, you pay for nothing to happen: not to sleep out under the beautiful stars; not to share the stories, the frenzies, and the fleas of the dockworkers' dormitory; to sit your buttocks—as I did the day before yesterday, out of fatigue—on the useless velvet of a compartment where the passengers across from you have been rendered so timid by education that they dare not or deign not speak a single word to you.

No more velvet here. This train—an engine with a bronze bell that trails its flourish of pearly smoke across the night, plus a single car—looks like the local lumbermen built it themselves with their knowledge of schoolbook rules (inertia, friction, pi equals 3.14, boiler compression) that saved the shipwreck survivors in *The Mysterious Island*. The poorly finished frames of the benches were still oozing resin, and you almost expected this wild little convoy to escape during switching and return whinnying to the forest from where it had come...

New stop: another station stuck in the great ice floe of sleep, a long way from Wakanai, which I will not reach tonight. The waiting room is freezing, and there isn't anywhere to get a meal in this place, which offers no more than turned black dirt, giant bell-shaped plants, piles of squared-off logs, animal dens, crows, and lonely lighthouses along a perpetually gray sea. I settle behind the ticket counter at the desk of the station chief, who seems to have gone to eat dinner at his mother's house. The assistant conductor counts and recounts the day's receipts on an abacus while munching on hazelnuts, offering me half of them. From time to time, he stops to break up an old "Suntory" whiskey box with his heels and feed it into a little cast-iron stove. Between additions, he tells me that since the beginning of the year, along the Wakanai line, bears have killed three calves, a horse, and a schoolboy and attacked two farmers, who drove them off with jabs from their pitchforks. The radio is tuned to a baseball game on the other side of the archipelago, but he is no longer listening, since he is now busy with an old woman in a scarf who has arrived several hours before her train and who has apparently not bought a round-trip ticket. She is worried, demanding, and won't listen to any of his answers. Rest assured, people can come as well as go. She won't believe it until she sees it. (Most of the people who came to live on this "island without memory" didn't do so of their own free will.) And besides, this certainty is a fairly recent luxury. In other times, poor people only traveled because they were forced to and went, their hearts heavy, to earn a meager living elsewhere. Often they had to go into debt or beg in order to leave, and then were faced with Indians, wolves, icebergs, runaway stagecoaches, the black plague, and Jesse Jameses besides. Hence this heartrending folklore about ports and stations that used to surround—and too often still does surround—the smallest trip. Silent families; women kissing the ground on the quay, standing among suitcases tied shut with string, full of bread and onions; faces disfigured by tears; and chapped hands waving handkerchiefs in the train's cinders or toward a mast swallowed by the round sea...

...The station chief returns, polishing his lantern. He is dumbfounded to find this foreigner seated at his table covered with scribbled sheets. He hesitates a moment between forced cordiality and cautiousness, regrets letting me see this hesitation, almost immediately looks for some way to oblige me. He telephones for a weather report, which he recites to me with a raised finger. *Ashta ga furi so desu*, it rained yesterday, and is raining today, and *will rain tomorrow*. A low pressure system has come in from the Kurils. So much the better! Rain in this country with so little, at least it adds a little bit of something more. Anyway, I'm very happy with a nature that doesn't play a symphony, just a few notes that it repeats incessantly. In this small range that reflects my own, I feel at home, I find myself, I have the feeling that I understand what it's trying to tell me. Besides, this station is starting to remind me of another station, in the Vaud canton (in Switzerland), where at the age of six or seven I often dozed, with my legs dangling, my face in my mittens, waiting for the milk train. Really! you say to me, this low, polar sky, this still sea, this absence, these crows—why the canton of Vaud? It's the light of this opaline lamp, counter-balanced, hanging too high above the table; the way the brown packages, securely tied with string, are heaped behind the ticket counter; the sound of this huge, round pendulum clock with hands as thick as a finger; in short, it is these nothings that team up and conspire to create an atmosphere. Since it is not by the identity of things in themselves, but by the relationships secretly established between them that allows places that seem to have nothing in common to suddenly resonate in a hallucinatory logic that is entirely new . . .

Four men in fur hats with profiles flattened out by the wind enter the waiting room and read manuals about repairing winches or sawing in the brown-sugar light—it is an aeolian wind that supplies the current. This is exactly how I pictured the "North" (native sleighs, pemmican) when I read a description of Hokkaidō in the *Journal des Voyages,* from 1894, a huge, bottle-green volume with tattered pages I was lent (call it "come back") by the switchman of the Allaman station, where I waited for the milk train. Milk cans, streetlamp halos, scarlet fever, tiny dancers in tutus in a music box. Six or seven years old . . .

. . . The train to Wakanai will arrive tomorrow morning. Leaning on the ticket counter, my chin firmly planted in my palms, I have been carried off to sleep, like a wisp of straw, in an outpouring of memories where everything, even the shadows, becomes mercifully minuscule.

WAKANAI

———————•———————

WHY HAVE I spent so much time talking about Hokkaidō,
where, admittedly, there is almost nothing?

First, because nobody talks about it; second, because in order to
digest the enormous Japanese meal, you have to retreat and take a
rest—for example, on this neglected island, which has only fog,
horses, green pastures, and emptiness . . . but this emptiness, how
restful!

In Wakanai, "historic density" is even more than diluted.

*It is the northernmost city of Japan, where one can see the Sakhalin moun-
tains on clear days. In the winter, the port does not freeze over because of the
warm Tsushima current that flows through the straits of Soya.* (Official
Japanese guide, 1962 edition)

A marine current—that's all they can find to say for this city!
Besides which, the sea is eternally gray, so this "attraction" is not
exactly noticeable. To give this town more importance, they
should have mentioned the weather station, which is on the air
continuously when they are anxiously watching a typhoon's path.
In fact, this is a very nice city; and I am going to add to the guide.

When I arrived here, every part of Wakanai was decorated with
colored lights and huge paper lanterns for the Tanabata Matsuri,
the annual Festival of Two Stars, which is celebrated on August 7.
The streets were black with schoolchildren in uniform, their
cheeks shining like doorknobs, and with huge sleigh dogs, panting
from the heat, their tongues hanging out, while watching all the

fanfare, scout troops, gymnasts, and the municipal council—all in frock coats—smelling like codfish.

Be sure not to miss the post office, its back wall is covered with lively and inventive graffiti, which I regret I can't reproduce here. Go to the fishing port, and especially to the dockyard behind it, where hundreds of crows nest in the wonderfully colored hulks of wrecked ships and where a team of strapping young guys, towels knotted around their foreheads, tear down old ships with a blow-torch to get what can be saved. When I arrived there, around noon, they were finishing a game of baseball, their field a space between two tall worm-eaten hulls. They brought me a basin full of *choshu* (potato alcohol), which they passed around, and they confided to me that they had been putting money in a kitty for a year, in the hope of taking the *Trans-Siberian Express* someday and going to visit Europe. Tanabata Matsuri is an auspicious day to conceive male children; on the night of the celebration, every husband is supposed to make love to his wife. Needless to say, the bars were filled with husbands shrinking from their duty or drinking to muster courage. I waited for my night train in a Chinese restaurant packed with irresolute drinkers. Everyone here was very drunk and cordial, with the exception of the Cantonese cook, who was literally wild-eyed with homesickness. Because I didn't appear American, they thought I was Russian (this outdated Manichaeism still is in vogue down here) and asked me what I could possibly have come to see in this city without ancestors or cemeteries. I like Japanese cemeteries, but I also like these places without a past, where everything is still possible, this sea that doesn't go anywhere, these trawler hulls scraped by workers whistling tunelessly under the pale sun, and above all, this Trinity of Polar Dog, Horse, and Crow. At the word "crow," the drunkest among them spilled half his beer and started tapping the bottom of his glass against the table, singing:

Karasu
Karasu
Kansaburo

Oya no on
Wasurenai yo

Crow
Crow
Kansaburo
it's not good to forget
what you owe your parents

But I had been marked by Kyoto: I knew that unless I responded
with something, they'd take me for a boor. I took out my notebook, I wrote:

WAKANAI, NORTH JAPAN, SUMMER 1965

Since Saint Francis Xavier
all the crows of Hokkaidō speak Latin
One... two... three
they count the nails of the Cross
blaspheming abominably
on a sea without ears

City? Boards, cabins, fishing nets!
but this evening it is full of lanterns
from the Far North to the Far South
schoolchildren in black and oiled lamps
Unity for the empire!

The pork in this bistro tastes a lot like dog
the Chinese cook is too far from his China
he sees a dragon in every cabbage he slices
and drinks his stock, eyes looking elsewhere...

Just yesterday they poked out the eyes of the traveler.

But the horse was too fat and refused to fit in the poem, so I
stopped there. When I raised my nose, the sky had finished turning

into night and everything was strangely transformed. By the half-open door to the kitchen, I could see a family kneeling around a wooden pail cleaning sea cucumbers with hooks. It made a soft, slimy sound that turned the stomach. My neighbors had entered the second stage of drunkenness, where one forgets everything from the first; those who could still stared at me with round eyes; the others were asleep, their heads pillowed on their arms and their jacket sleeves blotting up the alcohol spilled on the table. I heard the whistle of my train, and I cleared out without further ado. It was the end of the country and the end of something.

Hokkaidō can mean "The Route to the North Sea."

THE GRAY NOTEBOOK

———————————●———————————

SOMETIMES, propelled by curiosity, I buy a French review, which costs the price of two meals, just to see what's happening in French literature. Last time, I was rewarded for my effort: I came upon a story by Gaston Chaissac, a self-taught man, who writes like the Douanier Rousseau painted but with more awkwardness and even more life. The story is about his train trip back to Brittany after his first visit to Paris. Paris had delighted and stimulated him so completely that, for a time, he was transfixed by all he saw. One by one, he describes the travelers who pass through his compartment. This "Thomas Goes on a Spree" unfolds in the yellow light of the train car, and it amused me that he found it so amusing. It is fresh as watercress, not cooked up at all. For example, you come across a description like this one: "She was fat. Her fur coat was half open, and the string bag of potatoes that hung down between her legs looked like the small balls of a bull." I enjoyed the whole story, and with the idea of writing to Mr. Gaston Chaissac, I consulted his biography, which the editor had written in a more polished style.

Evidently, he was dead.

More precisely, "wracked" by tuberculosis; he had died on the ground floor of an abandoned school, alone except for the woman who constantly quarreled with him. Period. Yet the editors—at least those in this review—were not ignorant of his misery, his bitterness, nor the existence of those cloth-covered notebooks that he filled with such curious writings. But they left him to stew in his blood like the gourmet's duck left to ferment in its own juices to enhance its flavor. Once a man is dead, the wine is ready to be sold. Someone buys up the vintage and hosts a "retrospective," since Gaston Chaissac also smoothed his style on pieces of slate and old scraps of jute mats given by pitiful neighbors.

All businesses are the same, but I cannot complain, since I too bought him cheap, five or six beautiful pages of Gaston Chaissac for three new French francs and fifty centimes; these days, that's a bargain, you should grab it.

Alas, the rest of the review wasn't from the same mold. A poetic tidbit started with these words: "The place doesn't fail to be ordinary. We're talking about the angle of a singularly peopled café . . . " I know this is a café that "doesn't fail to" inspire a deadly moping, believe me, since I read this poem attentively to the end. And what kind of French is that? I know that Valéry is a tough nut to crack, but all the same . . . A little farther on, in a critical piece on a hermetic poet, this sentence: "It's enough for a thought to look at a blank page and it becomes a book." A revelation! Luckily for you, my thoughts are not so blessed that way.

I found many more trifles of this sort. The Yves St. Laurent of literature in an impeccably cut Didot or Garamond. Jewels that are no bigger than a half-carat. I am well aware that these chroniclers and poets are overworked, have been forced to read and have read so much that they detest all books. I know that the competition is fierce, it costs money to live, the butcher is clamoring; then there are the bills, the car registration, the gas, etc. The gas especially: pay the gas first! Maybe you can get out of paying the rest. Think about it.

But it's the last time that I will buy a review. From now on, I'll do what the Japanese students do: they read standing up in bookstores, in narrow aisles, under dim lighting that is intended to discourage this practice. But nothing can discourage them—even Saint Simon, in aisle 7, is spotted with thumb prints from beginning to end.

NAKANO-KU, DECEMBER 1965

If you don't need to finish, you work much faster. The Chinese, who do so many things playfully, despite their stuffy airs, are never in a hurry to finish anything. If it catches their fancy to carve, in jade, one open latticework bowl inside another, they're perfectly well aware that the work might have to be finished by a son or nephew. So they turn their attention to other work—raising ducks, for example, packing eggs in baskets of dirt and going to sell them in another province, learning Sanskrit on the way, or ordering a coffin in a place where the coffins are particularly colorful, and finally drowning while crossing a river in flood. But the bowl of jade was finished without their awareness, and many other things were achieved at the same time: a moral treatise, or twenty poems written all at once in the shade of a tree, thanks to the bamboo writing case carelessly hung from their belt along with the snuff box (the writing is not put away solemnly, but in the same sack as the smoke, its true place).

But me, I have a small "writing room," a typewriter, and a few books that possess a fearsome number of the virtues I lack. Maybe I need to devise a uniform to give me courage. Naturally, faced with all this paraphernalia, I feel quite useless, so completely crushed I can barely hang on; often an evening ends with no work to show for it. On the other hand, when I'm doodling on metro tickets, or on the modest menus of restaurants with French pretensions and signs that proclaim "This restaurant has air con" (meaning air conditioning), or when I'm running after the last train, which I miss, I catch ideas the way others catch venereal diseases: without too much trouble and certainly without trying. They are the only ideas that interest me, but too often these pieces of paper are lost in the bottom of my pockets, stuck in my penknife and sliced up, or get soggy with perspiration, the ink blurred so that they can no longer be deciphered—God giveth and God taketh away—or I use them carelessly to jot down my address for a student that I will never see again. But, all the same, while emptying my pockets or my wallet, I occasionally save something—I might have interviewed a famous professor the day before; or visited a school where I waded through a hundred difficulties in order to photograph things that I thought were interesting and that were not (ordinary—but I didn't realize it): these four or five lines, here, are my only profits. This is my work, and what I do on the side (hasty conferences, articles full of expedients and artifice) is only to give me a little substance to throw off my shadow and not disappear completely.

THE GRAY NOTEBOOK

———————•———————

Pages on the road, 1966–1970

T HERE ARE SHEPHERDESSES who marry sons of kings, and there are people whose karma it is to spend their lives— whatever they may have done before—with dish towel in hand. I think about this while watching the owner of a small all-night café on the Nagasaki highway. His gray face looks just like a dish towel, or a handkerchief that has wiped away many tears, known the bottoms of many pockets, and been through many washes. His face is full of a wrinkled kindness. I also find the sign of continual hesitation in his gestures, caused by education, an exhausted distinction. It is evident that it comes from another life, and nothing in his childhood could have anticipated the percolator or the gasoline pumps. His parents or masters had never foreseen that he would end up here, wiping this small counter with a dish towel, mumbling in a dull voice. His beginnings hardly matter, whether a failed student or a teacher passed over for advancement after a quarrel with the trustees. What matters is that the dish towel he holds like a scepter was in his stars, and so life has brought them together. He seems to know it and finds it very comfortable. Certain of being in his rightful place, emerging from the crowd of elbows and shoulders, he is totally involved in the spectacle of his café and listens to his customers with an attention that one rarely encounters even in love. People are so unaccustomed to someone paying so much attention that after about five minutes they are already sharing their secrets. Leaning toward them, he takes everything in, sometimes waving his dish towel in agreement; and I wonder what feelings he picks up this way, what passion, sickness, or insufficiency of soul makes him so keenly interested?

ISLAND OF SHIKOKU, MAY 1966

Saint Kōbō Daishi, commonly known as Kūkai, adds to his vocation as a genuine saint that of magician, herbalist, builder of roads and bridges, calligrapher, bonesetter, and educator of the poor. He was the one who created the first Japanese primer (eighth century), and I always imagine him carrying his alphabet, letter by letter—like a carpenter carries wood—shoulders aching, to the farthest mountain villages, to these simple souls he dreams of civilizing. For the most part, you can count him a success, because today Japan is one of the most literate countries in the world, despite its damnable system of writing.

All the same, there are some corners—I will not say where—that he must have forgotten, where you encounter people so rough that they don't so much resemble other people as the things they cook or grow: black radishes, turnips, bread pulled from the oven. Besides, they almost never speak. I intend no disparagement by this observation.

This thought was inspired by a servant at the inn, who explained just now where sashimi comes from. She unsticks her enormous buttocks from her heels just a bit, spreading her arms to explain the notion of "big," and roars in a raspy voice, *Okina sakana* (a big fish). A bonita, then. The size and name of this type of animal —and you sense that she could not explain any further even to her own brother. But it's not exactly that she's mean, dirty, or unhappy. She is more rough-hewn. A rough outline of a voice, a face with eyes, nose, and mouth barely sketched in, like a child's drawing after he has been scribbling too long and has lost interest in the project. She has enormous red cheeks, a considerable tuft of frizzy black hair, and she chews this word *sakana* like a mouthful that she can't swallow. Nature didn't expend much effort making her, and gave her only three yen of expression, barely enough to fill a tiny face, but she must have eaten a lot, and gotten bigger than Heaven had foreseen, so that the few features she had disappeared when her scale changed.

KYŪSHŪ, APRIL 1970

Japan and especially the Japanese summer blunts the attention you bring to things and—after twelve hours of train travel—makes your spirit as flat as the faces that surround you. But small moments of brotherhood break through occasionally. And you have to start with the small moments before thinking of the big ones.

In the bus station at Hataka, in the morning half-light, behind the pink- and pistachio-colored coaches, an otherworldly voice came from behind a lemonade counter; it was plaintive, piercing, and it rose over the roar of motors, the bustle of departure, the little bursts of panic about forgotten packages. It was a recording of a Noh performance that the lemonade maker was playing on his portable tape deck, and he was listening, following the words with his fingers, while he waited for someone to get thirsty. You could picture the bent and stiff silhouettes of the actors, the calculated, almost narcotic awkwardness, the gestures and gliding steps accompanied by slow grumbling speeches. Nowhere else, never in real life does anyone move or speak like the actors of the Noh theater. From this, a simple aural or gestural allusion, comes its power to transport you to a different world, a space outside of yourself. The ice cream vendor next door had come to lean on the counter and read over the shoulder of the lemonade man. They were both transported, enraptured. The Japanese culture that we try to wrap up in discussions and explanations is only as impressive as it is spontaneous and "of the moment." This morning we were far from the erudite swooning that would ruin it. The whistle of my boat for Pusan covered this plaintive monotone for a moment. I must go.

Hakata, June 1970

GOOD-BYE

●────────────────

Kyoto, April 1966

I HAVE LIVED alone here now for three months, in a house where, contrary to Kipling's prophecy, East does meet West.

When I first saw this phalanstery, vast private rooms, libraries, conveniences of all sorts, in short, an excellent hotel for the price of a garret, I thought that Japanese students, coming from their dormitories, would be happy there. I was kidding myself: this freedom that I thought was "all for the best" appeared to them as a lack of guidance, a field that hadn't been cleared of mines. Every morning, in the stairway, I would see the program of their next seminar: "We mind the pressure of Western thinking," and I know what they mean.

From time to time, I get a letter from Europe.

"Your son won't speak Japanese anymore, but sometimes he dreams whole sentences and wakes up because he cannot understand them. He asks me: 'What is *ippai?*' (Very simple: a child says that when he is satisfied.) He was very happy with the marionettes that you sent him, especially the *kyutaro* (a phantom), but he didn't recognize the *ninja*. The country is a blur to him: I hate the idea that time is erased so quickly."

One moment, my little one: a *ninja,* a malevolent acrobat with searching eyes, covered to the nose by a black cape; he was a messenger, spy, or assassin for the lords of distant times, who employed him for all the secret jobs they couldn't give their samurai. A *ninja* could jump two times his height, could match sabers with the best, could pull a razor-sharp mace out of his huge sleeves and swing it in the face of his enemies; and he could climb a knotted rope faster than a spider. He could hide in a cupboard barely big enough for a lamb, ears to the wall, overhear the tiniest murmur, and expose the secrets of others to his master.

In the past, as today, the people of this country lived secretly: then they needed spies. It was generally a good job, and the *ninjas* learned it in the Shiga-ken schools (where you once fell in a pond, but you don't remember anymore) and dedicated more years to the study of spying than you have yet lived. There was a *ninja boom* on television, just before the James Bond craze. That, you do remember.

As for you, Eliane, you add: "Look at Kyoto for me, I miss it." You? Who often felt so foreign, exiled, and lost here? Astonishing, the magic of memory! The same magic that transforms the dead into dear inoffensive shadows. Now everything that weighed on you here is held at a distance, like the light scent of mourning floating among many other smells; you pull from your memory the images that please you and you patiently illuminate them, sometimes raising your eyes to the green fields of Europe. So books are written.

I will also, soon, miss this city, because it is unique, wonderful . . . and because I have lived here.

But now I'm here, like a cork on the black water, with a few sips of gin in front of me, and I'm looking: the city, dark and slushy with melting snow, is stretched out in this endless winter, like a big cold-blooded animal washed up by the sea. Never, not even in the worst moments of March, has it seemed so sad to me: an immense school full of tired and submissive students; full of shadows; full of base things that mean little and go nowhere, that you must forget in order to return to life. Yellow heads, wise and knowing, and my head swollen and sore from poorly understood lessons.

This morning, a friend found this for me in the Jerusalem Bible: "Then there was a violent earthquake, and the sun went black as a sack of horsehair, and the moon became as red as blood, and the stars of Heaven fell to earth like aborted figs showering from the branches of a tree bowed by the wind, and the sky disappeared like a scroll rolling up . . ."

In the past, this city was full of silk, blood, domesticated

daydreams for the diversion of ladies-in-waiting, painters who paused, with brush poised, for the light or the wind to reveal the ultimate form of things; it was full of haunting memories, insomniacs, and sacred texts to be hurled like reinforcements in the heat of a quarrel, and of true, good moments reclaimed from death. Today, the sky has been rolled up and a black canvas rolled down. Rather than a root, tradition is a lid, and a tight-fitting one. I live in a great collection of wonders that respect has poisoned to death. Not far from here, in the Tenri sect, every evening someone still prepares the meal and the bath of a founder—dead for sixty years. There is a bit of this in Kyoto; and under these trailing snow clouds, this kind of gloomy masquerade seems more clear to me than ever. This evening, even the little Buddhas at the crossroads, usually so helpful and benevolent, have crooked mouths and seem to hang their heads under the burden of imposture and obligation. But I am getting carried away: I'm talking like a protester at Kyodai (the imperial university of Kyoto). I have become very Japanese!...I was also struck this morning, for the first time, by an aspect of the city that interests and touches me: it evokes the old erudite Jewish world of Europe in the nineteenth century, reminiscent of the Judeo-Goethean academism of the publishers and bookstores of Leipzig: glasses slipping down the nose, interminable delays for little things, which are—as everyone knows— the mother of important things, a smooth way of talking, a subtle and aphoristic humor, a collector's memory, huge and pillowy; and behind these entrenchments, certificates, and loopholes lies a crystalline liberty, a lesson of all and nothing that I have learned very poorly. It is time for me to pick up my knapsack and go live somewhere else.

TRANSLATOR'S ACKNOWLEDGMENT

I would like to give a special thanks to both the developmental editor, Carol Christensen, and the copyeditor, Alice Klein, for their unflagging attention to detail and experienced editorial guidance.

I wish to thank Sharon Smith for her beautiful cover, Hazel White for her constant supervision throughout all aspects of production, and Thomas Christensen for his editorial vision and faith. I thank publisher Bill Brinton and all the Mercury House staff for their support and hard work.

Finally, I wish to thank Dan for the home-cooked meals, the readings, the encouragement. I dedicate this translation to you.

ABOUT THE AUTHOR

"The traveler," writes Nicolas Bouvier, "is always an enigma. He is at home everywhere and nowhere. His is a life of stolen moments, reflections, minute sensations, chance discoveries, and odds and ends."

Nicolas Bouvier was born in Geneva in 1929 and educated at Geneva University, where he received master's degrees in history, literature, and law. He roamed the world for many years as a journalist and photographer—to Lapland, Central Europe, the Sahara, Turkey, Iran, Pakistan, India, Sri Lanka, China, and Japan. Bouvier spent the most extended period of time in Japan: in 1955 and 1956, when he worked at odd jobs and free-lance assignments for Japanese cultural magazines; in 1964 to 1966, on assignment for *Éditions Rencontré;* and in 1970, as a writer and photographer at the Osaka World Exhibition.

Bouvier's first book, *L'Usage du Monde* (1963), has become the bible of a new generation of travel writers. *Le Poisson-Scorpion* (1982) won the Critics' Prize. *The Japanese Chronicles* was chosen by *Lire* magazine as one of the best books of 1989 and was awarded the Librarians' Prize of 1989. Now a resident of Cologny, Switzerland, Bouvier is currently the photo editor for the Swiss magazine *Le Temps Stratégique* and a free-lance television and radio journalist.